A Chapter Guide to Gene Wolfe's Smithe Novels

Michael Andre-Driussi

Sirius Fiction

To Roy C. Lackey

CONTENTS

INTRODUCTION

This work is a chapter-by-chapter reading guide to Gene Wolfe's "Smithe" novels of science fiction mystery: *A Borrowed Man* (2015) and *Interlibrary Loan* (2020).

The Guide is intended to be used by first time readers of each book as well as those who are rereading them. The idea is that we are reading together, you and I. There are no spoilers, but things will be noted as they are revealed.

Each chapter has a synopsis followed by notes. Because these novels are mysteries, the synopsis will often be light on details to avoid spoiling mysteries. The notes are largely "literary" in nature, giving details from reviews, pointing to similarities in other works of fiction, giving the onomastic "meaning of names" where available, and flagging anomalies. There are also notes on Geography and Economics.

After the final chapter of each novel is a set of appendices made up of timelines and brief articles.

How To Use The Guide

A reader could read a chapter of the source text first, then check in this book for the notes.

Or

A reader who has already read the entire source text might read this book directly.

∆∆∆

Wolf in the OED

Using the brute force method, here are some applications of "wolf" to watch for, from the *Oxford English Dictionary:*

wolf: a kind of fishing net

"a hair of the same wolf" (like "hair of the dog that bit you")

"a wolf in sheep's clothing"

to throw to the wolves

lone wolf

Wolfland: former name for Ireland

wolfpen: strong box made of logs, used for trapping wolves

wolf-willow

Notes on this corrected edition: When I moved to make a small correction to the first page, I discovered that programs had changed, or something. As a result, I had to make larger design changes. Removing part pages and reformatting the bibliography reduced the page count.

A BORROWED MAN

Edition cited: Tor (hb), ISBN 978-0-7653-8114-9, 2015, 300 pp.

Dedication: "For my British friend, Nigel Price"

Commentary: Nigel Price and Jonathan Laidlow in 2000 established the website "Ultan's Library" as a resource to support the study of Gene Wolfe's work. "Ultan's Library" presents not only new articles, but also older, hard to find items, such as Jeremy Crampton's fanzine "The Book of Gold" (1988–89) and at least two pieces written for John Clute's proposed Wolfe book (1988–92), those pieces being Crampton's "Some Greek Themes in Gene Wolfe's Latro Novels" and my own "The Death of Catherine the Weal and Other Stories."

Nigel Price spent time with Gene Wolfe during the days of at least one convention near Chicago and even received a private meeting with Wolfe away from the convention.

1. From the Spice Grove Public Library (9–26)

E. A. Smithe is a young man with an old man's body, a reclone of a mystery author from a century before. He is programmed with memories from the brainscans of the original.

He lives on a public library shelf in New America. He is writing on a borrowed screen, an item he is not supposed to have. Writing is forbidden for him, yet he is somehow getting around that in composing this tale.

The adventure begins when a fully human woman named Colette Coldbrook checks him out. She needs him to solve a mystery related to a book his original wrote. Flying in a hovercab from Spice Grove toward Taos Towers, Colette suddenly changes the plan, and they are dropped off at a ruined garden.

Smithe tells her that his original married a poet named Arabella Lee, but the marriage only lasted two years before she divorced him (19).

Colette shows Smithe the book, but since he does not recognize it, he thinks it was written after the original Smithe's last brain scan. Colette says she talked to experts on codes and ciphers (24).

Silent E: James Wynn, in his review "A Weird Mystery" at "Ultan's Library" notes that a "silent E" adorns the surname of both hero and author.

Hammett: Dashiell Hammett is a towering figure of the mystery genre. A few Hammett mysteries start with a beautiful female client hiring the detective, the most famous being the Sam Spade novel *The Maltese Falcon* (1930). But Smithe is no Sam Spade, since Spade works the familiar ground of his home town. Because Smithe is thrust into an unknown territory, he is more like Hammett's earlier hero, the unnamed Continental Op, who often pursues cases in places he had never been before, like "Corkscrew" (1925), an Arizona cowboy mystery, and "The King Business" (1928), set in the Balkans.

Onomastics: James Wynn points out that the name "E. A. Smithe" looks to be a blend of two names from authors known to be among Wolfe's favorites: Edgar Alan Poe and Clark Ashton Smith. (Poe is considered a father of the mystery genre, whereas Smith did not write in that mode.) For our hero, the E is for "Ern," and this is usually taken as being a variant on the German Earnest, meaning "Earnest," "Serious," "Determined," or "Vigor." The surname "Smithe" is an occupational name.

For Colette Coldbrook, "Colette" is French for "Necklace" or Greek for "People's Victory," and "Coldbrook" is a locational name, and also the name of an unincorporated community in Illinois.

For Arabella Lee, "Arabella" is German for "Eagle Heroine," and "Lee" is a meadow or forest clearing. Wolfe uses the name Arabella in the novel *Peace* (1975) for a ghost-chasing journalist, sister to Adelina, and aunt to narrator Alden Denis Weer.

Apollo: In the novel *Zanoni* (1842) by Edward Bulwer-Lytton, a character divines an Apollonian linkage to the surname Smith(e), saying,

> the numerous family of Smiths in England were undoubtedly the ancient priests of the Phrygian Apollo. "For," said he, "was not Apollo's surname, in Phrygia, Smintheus? How clear all the ensuing corruptions of the august name,—Smintheus, Smitheus, Smithe, Smith! And even now, I may remark that the more ancient branches of that illustrious family, unconsciously anxious to approximate at least by a letter nearer to the true title, take a pious pleasure in writing their names Smithe!" (Chapter 2.VII)

Poe: Arabella Lee is close to "Annabel Lee" (1849), the last complete poem by Poe. Published posthumously, its narrator pines for his wife who died young, and expresses his hope of seeing her again.

People from Books: In the 1970s a trope arose in genre about beings or simulations from texts. In Michael Davidson's *The Karma Machine* (1975) there was a brief mention of educational androids, each programmed with all the text of a given sacred figure. Wolfe touched on this exact point in his novella "The Doctor of Death Island" (1978): "To have found it [speaking pages] in the Bible did not . . . so much surprise him—the temptation to chat with Christ would be irresistible" (*The Island of Doctor Death and Other Stories and Other Stories,* 254). Pushing further, John Crowley's *Engine Summer* (1979) explored people from books as tragic prisoners of stories they could not know.

Anomalies: Flying in a hovercab from Spice Grove toward Taos Towers they move from twilight into day in minutes, which is odd, since it is 2 PM, far too early for twilight (in Summer, using Kansas City as an example, sunset comes around 7:30 PM, beginning Civil Twilight). Moving from twilight into daylight suggests moving up high enough to see the sun clear of the horizon, or moving west enough to do the same by changing time zones. Perhaps this oddity resolves by making the "twilight" a localized shadow cast by big buildings around the library, with the noted change caused by the hovercab gaining altitude so that normal 2 PM daylight is achieved.

Economics: The ten-day rental deposit for Smith is 4,700 (16). The hovercab says he can buy out of his servitude with another 34,000 (17), and he plans on going humanoid, gaining a life-like, robotic body (17–18).

Geography: Smithe can see mountains from Spice Grove, but they are never named, nor is their direction established. If they are the Rockies, then Spice Grove is within 100 miles east of the Rockies. As an example, the Rocky Mountains are visible from Fort Morgan, Colorado (40º north, 103º west), at a distance of about 100 miles.

2. Colette's Story (27–37)

Colette tells Smithe about her family. She had a brother, two years older, named Conrad Junior. Her mother died, and Colette plans to reclone her. A few years later her father died. He had been a financial consultant with his own newsletter.

Colette tells Smithe that after her father Conrad died, her brother Cob discovered a hidden safe, which he showed her after the funeral. Her brother was murdered a few days ago, shortly after giving her the book that was the only thing in the safe.

The book is *Murder on Mars.* Smithe now remembers writing it as a small press side project.

Smithe reads a couple selections of the book and quotes a poem by his wife Arabella:

> One by one across the desert
> Until our boots grow too heavy with
>   The sands of time. (36)

Taking the case, Smithe has an epiphany about himself as rising to this challenge as a real detective.

Imitation Life Imitates Art: The first line of *Murder on Mars* goes like this: "He was neither angel nor devil, but something for which we have only bad words or none, a being young and ancient, neither good nor evil, who knew too well the roads to the farther stars" (31). The bit about being simultaneously "young and ancient" fits reclone Smithe very well.

Clark Ashton Smith: Wolfe-trackers will recall Wolfe's enthusiasm for Smith's "dying sun" stories set in far-future Zothique, but Smith also wrote a few tales set upon Mars ("The Vaults of Yoh-Vombis" (1932), "The Dweller in the Gulf" (1932), and "Vulthoom" (1935)). Smith's Martian tales focus on subterranean horrors, very similar to this quote from the middle of *Murder on Mars:*

> Eridean had called them the sewers, but they were enormously larger and more varied than the term implied, tunnels and cellars and subcellars and worse, far beneath the city. There were animals in them, he knew. Animals, men more hostile and more fell than any beast, and plants that throve without the sun, pale growths that feasted upon the living and the dead. Yet what Apolean met was none of these, but a woman. (32)

The names "Eridean" and "Apolean" sound Smithian (and the hero's name sounds quite Apollonian). On the other hand, Smith's heroes exploring Mars never meet a woman, so that is different, and seems more like Smith's "The Isle of the Torturers" (1933), or in literature, the golden bough episode of Virgil's *Aeneid,* where the Sibyl of Cumae guides Aeneas in the underworld. A Smith story that explicitly enumerates multiple subterranean levels is "The Seven Geases" (1933). Smith did not write any novels.

H. Beam Piper: Perhaps because I detect a certain amount of H. Beam Piper in Wolfe's first novel, *Operation ARES* (1970), another Piper detail pops up for me here: while Piper is known for being the author of several science fiction books, his first published novel was a mystery, *Murder in the Gunroom* (1953). So *Murder on Mars* seems to be a genre-flipped oddity like *Murder in the Gunroom,* blended with Clark Ashton Smith's version of Mars.

3. What We Did (38–50)

Back to the hovercab, which estimates the trip to Taos Towers will take two or three hours (40).

Colette suspects her brother Cob was murdered for the book.

In Colette's apartment, two sinister men visit at 11 PM (42). They demand the book, saying it belongs to them and that Cob stole it. They say Cob gave it to Colette.

But Smithe had hidden it. The men beat them, tie them up, ransack the place, and leave. Smithe reveals to Colette that he had dropped the book down the laundry chute.

Smithe falls asleep reading the book and has a monster-fighting nightmare.

Onomastics: For the romance writer Rose Romain (49), "Rose" is the flower name, and "Romain" is the French form of "Roman."

Geography: Taos Towers is still in Spice Grove (49), patrolled by the Spice Grove Police Department (43). Three hours of hovercab travel seems like a long way, but the text does not say how fast hovercabs fly. If it is 55 mph/90 kph, three hours would be 165 miles/270 km. That seems like the radius of an imperial city, or the scale of a Big Empty.

New Delphi is southeast of Spice Grove (49).

4. Her Father's House (51–57)

The Coldbrook place is a country mansion. She tells him that she and her brother had rooms on the second floor.

They tour the hangar, enter the house by the rear door, and go through the kitchen. In the sunroom they pause to view the family portrait on their way to the lift tube.

Dickens: After listing some titles, Smithe says, "You'd like to ask him [Dickens] how he really felt about Kate, and about that actress. How he had intended to finish *Edwin Drood*—and so would I" (53).

"Kate" is Catherine Hogarth Dickens, wife to Charles Dickens and mother of his children. "That actress" is Ellen Ternan, the mistress of Dickens from 1858 to his death in 1870. *The Mystery of Edwin Drood* is the novel Dickens was working on when he died. It is an incomplete murder mystery, which makes it a double mystery.

Buck Rogers: Colette's flitter seems like a vehicle from Buck Rogers, especially the way the cabin separates in two. (The mansion's "lift tube" initially sounds like a Buck Rogers device, an anti-gravity shaft, but further details make it merely a smart elevator of the *Star Trek* variety.)

The Buck Rogers comic strip was avidly read by young Gene Wolfe, as he told Larry McCaffery in a 1988 interview:

> "I had a very nice grandmother . . . who used to save me the Sunday comics so that when I visited her there would always be a huge stack of Sunday funnies. I read those with particular attention to Buck Rogers and Flash Gordon." (Wright's *Shadows of the New Sun*, p. 80)

Wolfe makes reference to Buck Rogers in his poems "Oh God Mother I Want To Ride The Turtle's Back Again" and "British Soldier near Rapier Antiaircraft Missile Battery Scans for the Enemy."

To the text at hand, Buck Rogers was accidentally catapulted into the future, just as Smithe has been. Buck found an America depopulated and changed in many fundamental ways, just as Smithe has. Buck was initially guided in this world by a flying woman, just as Smithe has been.

5. On the Fourth Floor (58–74)

The fourth floor has three doors, one to the lab. Colette says the key card to the lab had been on Conrad's body, among the effects turned over by the mortuary, and after Cob used it, he left the lab door unlocked (61).

Smithe hears details about Cob climbing up the outside of the house to windows on the forbidden fourth floor. He has Colette order a copy of *Murder on Mars,* but the response is "No such title." He finds a cache of scientific articles and proposes Colette call the author K. Justin Roglich (71). Through this action he is hoping to draw out the sinister men.

Colette says her father died in his early fifties (67). Six days after the funeral, the will was read, then Cob was murdered two weeks later (68).

Colette tells about their being tied up after Smithe was knocked out.

Wolfeana: Colette has violet eyes (63), a recurring pattern seen in such cases as young Phaedra in "The Fifth Head of

Cerberus" (1972), Aunt Olivia in *Peace* (1975), and exultant Thecla in *The Shadow of the Torturer* (1980).

Wolfe often has significant characters at or around 23 years of age: Agia and Severian in *New Sun*, Silk in *Long Sun*. In *A Borrowed Man*, Colette and Cob are both under age 30 (63). Since Colette says she thinks Smithe is 22 years old (20), this might mean she is 23 years old. She could be younger, or older, so 23 years old ±2 years.

Geography: Birgenheier is the college or university at Owenbright (66).

Niagara seems to be the capital of New America (67). Remarkable in the text for being a recognizable place name.

Economics: Colette says the house was appraised at 2,500,000 (69).

Allusion: A wise old general about how your enemy is not infinite in men or ammo (73).

6. Back On The Shelf (75–89)

Smithe and Colette visit Dr. Roglich, astrophysicist, in Owenbright. Colette says that her father died six weeks ago (76). Roglich says he spoke with Conrad about the fundamental nature of space. After a while, Roglich directs Smithe to find the eavesdropping bug in the office, which Smithe destroys. Roglich describes the two sinister men being accompanied by a woman, a new figure. The interview ends at 5 PM (84).

Colette and Smithe rent connected rooms at a local hotel. Colette is abducted while Smithe is in the shower.

After a frustrating call to the police, Smithe turns himself in at the Owenbright Public Library.

Onomastics: For K. Justin Roglich from (Latin) "Justus" meaning "Just," "Fair," "Righteous," and "roglich" is a Bavarian word meaning "loose, shaking." Notice how Dr. Roglich is shaking, true to his name.

Geography: Since they take a hovercab to Owenbright (84), this might suggest Owenbright is fairly close to New Delphi.

7. "Where's E. A. Smithe?" (90–101)

The next morning at the library, Smithe is having breakfast

beside a reclone of historian Johnston Biddle when he is found by Arabella, a reclone of his ex-wife, a poet. (Her voice is the voice he had heard before sleeping.)

Later in the day, Smithe meets a little blond man who gives him 300 yellowbacks (creds), buys him sandwiches, and talks about getting him out. He says he works for the tall man (of the two sinister men), then leaves.

A 'bot collects Smithe for shipping back to the Spice Grove Public Library.

Onomastics: For Johnston Biddle, "Johnston" is "John's town," and "Biddle" is from (Old English) personal name "Bita," or from "Beadle" for a person of authority.

Hammett: The witty patter between Ern and Arabella echoes the snappy banter between husband-and-wife team Nick and Nora Charles, introduced in the novel *The Thin Man* (1934). Two of Hammett's most famous characters, they developed a life of their own in a series of six motion pictures from 1934 to 1947.

Curious Quote: Arabella, on her preference for anger over sadness, says, "'Great wit is unto madness near allied.' Who said that?" (94). Setting aside the fact that she is mismatching madness for anger, Smithe guesses it was Shakespeare, but it is actually Alexander Pope. "Great wit is unto madness near allied, And thin partitions do their bounds divide."

Dr. Johnson: Smithe, being tempted with food by the blond man, tries to remember "the name of the boy Dr. Johnson had talked about, the young genius who had choked to death on a sweet roll" (97). This cryptic allusion is about Thomas Otway (1651–1685), an English dramatist of the Restoration period, a genius who died at age 33. Dr. Johnson wrote about him in *Lives of the English Poets, Volume 7,* including the sad story of his demise:

> Having been compelled by his necessities to contract debts, and hunted, as is supposed, by the terriers of the law, he retired to a publick house on Tower hill, where he is said to have died of want; or, as it is related by one of his biographers, by swallowing, after a long fast, a piece of bread which charity had supplied. He went out, as is reported, almost naked, in the rage of hunger, and, finding a

gentleman in a neighbouring coffee-house, asked him for a shilling. The gentleman gave him a guinea; and Otway, going away, bought a roll, and was choked with the first mouthful.

Dr. Johnson also noted that Alexander Pope wrote a different theory about Otway's death, that his sudden death was due to fever, "caught by violent pursuit of a thief that had robbed one of his friends."

Economics: The cash gift to Smithe is 300 (98).

8. On the Route Truck (102–17)

Smithe bargains with the fully human driver to improve his lot. The next day they drop off two books at a small-town library. Smith puzzles over the fuzzy nature of when Conrad died (105); Cob's behavior (105–106); and the behavior of the sinister men (106).

Lunch finds them at a university library where they pick up another Arabella Lee reclone, this one being sent to a library at Inspiration. Smithe tells the amused driver about their two years of marriage (109).

Upon arrival at the Spice Grove Public Library, Smithe learns that two men want to check him out the next day.

Genre: Smithe identifies *Murder on Mars* as a fantasy murder (104).

Economics: Smithe's meal allowance is six creds (102).

Geography: The route seems to be from New Delphi to Spice Grove. The distance from Inspiration to Spice Grove is 450 km/280 miles (114).

Original Life: At one point, Smithe writes how he was "jouncing along in that truck and looking out at all that was left of one of the old cities where I used to live" (106). Sounds specific, but might be generic.

Anomalies: "Fortunately, the night was warm" (114) is certainly different from the night before, which was cold enough that Smithe bought a warm blanket. "[F]ive hours of actual travel" (114) and 450 km of distance means an average speed of 90 kph (which is 56 mph). However, walking "ten weeks or more" (115) equals 70 days, and 450 km divided by 70 days equals 6.4 km a day, a paltry 4 miles. Smithe's numbers are off, probably due to his lack of life experience.

Onomastics: For cookbook author Millie Baumgartner (116), "Millie" means "Industrious," and "Baumgartner" (German) means "Tree Gardner."

For E. A. Smithe, he reaches a bedrock truth in the root of trouble between himself and Arabella, that mysteries sell while poetry does not (112). This, in turn, puts a new twist on his first name, moving away from "earnest" to "earning." The original Smithe was clearly an "earning author," so perhaps to complete this pun his middle name is "Arthur."

9. Payne, Fish, and Pain (118–37)

Smithe interrupts his narrative to outline his implanted mental block against writing. His solution is to write the way he thinks, not the way his conditioning makes him speak.

Smithe is checked out by SGPD officers Payne and Fish. They are apparently not the two who were asking to check him out before. They take him to a safehouse for questioning, where he tells them about *Murder on Mars* containing some sort of secret. They beat him. After midnight he breaks out and escapes.

Frame Tale: "I'm not sure how you back up on this [device]" (118). In composing this novel, Smithe is alternating between keyboard and speech (119). Technically, he is also reporting true experiences rather than creating fiction, which provides another possible work-around to his conditioning.

Poe: Poe's C. Auguste Dupin, the prototype of all fictional detectives, has two distinct personas. In his first adventure, "The Murders in the Rue Morgue" (1841), when Dupin is relating details of his exact examination:

> His manner . . . was frigid and abstract; his eyes were vacant in expression; while his voice, usually a rich tenor, rose into a treble . . . Observing him in these moods, I often dwelt meditatively upon the old philosophy of the Bi-Part Soul, and amused myself with the fancy of a double Dupin—the creative and the resolvent.

There is great argument over what, exactly, Poe meant by "Bi-Part Soul," yet Smithe is similar for having two distinct voices, his highly conditioned speaking voice versus his writing voice.

Technology: The hovercraft used is like a hovercab, but it never flies "anywhere near as high" (119).

Interrogation Tips: "Describe the mother" (124). At first, this focus on the Coldbrook mother seems significant. With further thought, however, the first questions of a trained interrogation are not likely to be very important at all.

Alchemy: Officer Payne says of Conrad, "Somebody said once that he could pull gold out of the air" (129).

10. Road Trip (138–54)

Smithe decides to go overdue. He hits upon the idea that Colette is in New Delphi, because that is where so much of the mystery is centered (140). He goes to the bus station to buy a ticket to New Delphi. During the day-long ride he meets a poor couple, Georges Fevre and Mahala. They are taking the bus to New Delphi because "It's bigger than Spice Grove" (149).

Shortly before arriving at New Delphi, the bus passes the Coldbrook mansion (149), so it is located along the route connecting New Delphi to Spice Grove.

It is a rainy night when they arrive at Spice Grove. Smithe bribes the needy house van driver to take the three of them to the Coldbrook mansion.

As they enter the house, they hear Colette speak, then scream.

Pinocchio: "It was hero time" (139). Smithe sees opportunity for validation. He is like Pinocchio on his quest to become a real boy.

Puss in Boots: Smithe compares himself to the cat hero by name (140). This is something of a downshift from Pinocchio, but perhaps more heroic.

Emeralds: "I'm not going to say a whole lot about the bus trip . . . because those things do not really have much of anything to do with the emeralds or cutting Colette loose from the guy that had taken her" (143).

Economics: Paying for the bus ticket (and the blanket, and the meals on the route truck trip) seems to have used up most of the 300 creds the blond man had given Smithe (145). Smithe dips into the Colette money to give the driver a twenty-five cred note (153).

Silent E: "Fevre" ends with a silent E, suggesting some kinship with Smithe.

Onomastics: For Mahala, "Mahala" is a Hebrew name for girls. It is taken as "tender," but it really means sickness or disease. For Georges Fevre, "Georges" is the French form of "George," from the Greek name meaning "farmer," and "Fevre" is French for "fever," but the French surname "Lefèvre" is an occupational name for an ironworker or "Smith." Additional kinship with Smithe.

Geography: The route from Spice Grove to New Delphi has stops at Rapid Rivers and Hapigarden (142). The bus sets out at 5 AM, arrives at Rapid Rivers at noon (144), and Hapigarden at 2 PM (147). Seven hours at 55 mph equals 385 miles (Spice Grove to Rapid Rivers), and two hours at 55 mph equals 110 miles (Rapid Rivers to Hapigarden).

11. A Lonely House in the Rain (155–69)

Searching the house, they find no people, but there are still the two locked doors on the fourth floor. Georges figures the bad guys dragged Colette out the back door and into a ground car or a flitter.

In the yard by the garage they discover a car. Inside the garage they discover the mansion's robots, sent there by Colette. The maid 'bot gives information that contradicts the timeline established by Colette, suggesting that Conrad was still alive when Cob was murdered: that the 'bot was purchased by Conrad shortly before Cob's death (162); that Conrad told Colette not to speak of Cob's death (163); that Conrad told the 'bot to clean the floor where Cob's corpse was found (164).

Since this contradicts the earlier story, Smithe has Mahala use a screen to find Merciful Maids. That shows no such company, so he has her find Colette's friend Bettina John, who denies having recommended a maid service as Colette had said. Smithe is shocked when Bettina says the Coldbrooks had servants after the mother died (166).

Privately Smithe uses a screen to research Georges and Mahala. He finds Mahala Levy had escaped institutionalization. He deduces that Georges is actually George G. Franklin of the High Plains Police, fired from the force and divorced shortly afterward.

Flitter Technology: Georges says, "So whoever it is that's holding the girl may have a flitter, too . . . If they do, they could be in Afasia before midnight" (156). "Afasia" seems to be a term for the combined landmass of Africa, Europe, and Asia. If this is true, Georges is saying that a flitter can reach Europe within six hours.

Buck Rogers: Missile pistols (160–61) are clear items from Buck Rogers, but historically there is also the Gyrojet family of rocket rifles and pistols developed in the 1960s.

Onomastics: For George Franklin, "Franklin" means "Free." For Mahala Levy, "Levy" is usually from the Hebrew surname "Levi," the line of priests, but another way is from the Irish "Mac Duinnshléibhe," meaning "Son of Donn of the Mountain." Anglicized as "MacDonlevy," and then shortened into Levy, Levey, Leevy, and Leavy.

Geography: "High Plains" is a geographical term for a distinctive terrain type in North America, east of the Rockies, between the 96th and 98th meridians, forming a band about 100 miles wide, from eastern Montana to the Texas panhandle.

Couple on the Run: Georges and Mahala have a mystery about them. He is an ex-cop; she is a fugitive from a eugenics program. Because he comes from "High Plains," it seems like they first traveled north or south to Spice Grove, then southeast to New Delphi.

12. Behind Locked Doors (170–89)

Waking up, Smithe goes to a corner room, where he climbs out the window and goes up one floor, entering the fourth floor through a window. He finds the first locked room contains a nuclear reactor. He goes back out the window, finds a window to another room, and looks into a jungle.

He enters the jungle and finds the door to the fourth floor of the mansion.

At breakfast he tells Georges a bit and learns that Georges worked nuclear reactors out of college.

Smithe and Georges discuss the possibility of a second key to the locked doors (178).

In the lab, Mahala hands over a dozen receipts for emeralds (181), reinforcing what Smithe had seen before (67). Smithe recalls Colette had mentioned emeralds when telling about Cob giving her the book (30).

Smithe uses the book *Murder on Mars* to open the locked door to the jungle planet, and the three of them go through.

Smithe believes the kidnappers brought Colette to this world when the trio heard the scream.

They think this part is a small island.

They hear drumming and smell smoke.

Hanging Gardens: Wolfe's fiction often has rooftop gardens, which I now designate as echoes of the legendary Hanging Gardens of Babylon, a wonder of the ancient world.

Heinlein: The doorway to another planet evokes *Tunnel in the Sky* (1955), a novel about a group of students teleported to another planet as their final exam.

Clark Ashton Smith: The short story "The Door to Saturn" (1932) is named for a wizard's escape hatch, leading from Earth to another world.

13. Rented in Owenbright (190–204)

On the jungle island, they discover a group of humanoid creatures in a ceremony. When these natives see the trio, they immediately give chase.

Smithe theorizes that Conrad's likely interaction with the humanoids is a possible explanation for his long absence from Earth (191). That the long absence had been a mistake rather than a plan. "That mistake may have been at the root of all the problems" (191).

Back on Earth, Georges shows Smithe details about the reactor, saying it is probably five or six years old (193). Georges points out that the lab safe uses a combination lock with 36 buttons (197). Georges reveals car-stealing techniques and unlocks the strange ground car. At 1 PM they discover it was rented in Owenbright to Colette Carole Coldbrook. Smithe explains Colette's abduction to them and realizes that Colette had escaped her captors and rented the car to return here. Mahala searches for Coldbrooks and Caroles in New Delphi (203).

Alone, Smithe goes back to the other world and examines the mine there, finding a missile rifle (204).

Silent E: The silent E at the end of surname "Carole" suggests a kinship to Smithe.

Onomastics: Colette's middle name is Carole (202), and "Carole" is "Free Person" or "Song."

Wolfeana: Mention of "Niagara" as a transit hub (203), and before as the presumed capital of New America (67), brings another Wolfe story into play, "The Eyeflash Miracles" (1976), collected in *The Island of Doctor Death and Other Stories and Other Stories*. In this novella, Niagara is the capital (IODD, 353), where there is an Office of Biogenetic Improvement (IODD, 355), and the story involves an agent hunting down a "defective" who is blind.

In "The Eyeflash Miracles" the agent hunting the defective is named "George," and he refers to himself as a farmer, but he goes by a number of aliases.

14. Maxette, Money, Monsters, and a Moon (205–22)
Mahala finds Alice Carole, mother of Joanne Rebecca Carole Coldbrook, and urges her to report Colette as missing. She also locates Judy Peters, former housekeeper (205).

The trio takes the seven uncut emeralds Smithe found at the mine to one of the jewelers Conrad had dealt with. This jeweler claims to have never met Cob (210); he also says he saw Conrad after Cob's death (211). After a lot of haggling, they sell six of the emeralds.

In the middle of the night, Smithe goes to the other world to get the missile rifle. While exploring the beach, he sees no scarecrow creatures, and he hides the book. Then there is something large out in the sea coming towards him. A lot of smaller creatures come off of it and they chase Smithe.

After he escapes, he sits on the beach and thinks about the alien moon, noting that it is whiter than ours, probably due to ice (220–21). Then he thinks about the burning room at the library, and the video he had seen of a burning (222).

Onomastics: For Alice Carole, "Alice" is Old German "Noble" and "Exalted," and "Carole" is "Free Person" or "Song."

For Joanne Rebecca Carole Coldbrook, "Joanne" is Hebrew for "God is Gracious," "Rebecca" is Hebrew for "Moderator" (from a word for join, tie, snare).

For Judy Peters, "Judy" is Hebrew for "Praised," and "Peters" is "Son of Peter," where "Peter" is famously "Stone."

Frame Setting: "which maybe I have written about here before" (216); "Here in the library" (221).

15. Some Errands in New Delphi (223–40)
Smithe retrieves the book and returns to Earth. The Coldbrook garage has three cars: "a classy limo, a sleek red convertible, and a big alterrain" (226). The trio takes the red, returns the rental car, buys a temp eephone for Smithe, then visits Mrs. Judy Peters, the former housekeeper of the Coldbrook mansion.

Mrs. Peters had worked that job for three years. It was back when Mrs. Coldbrook had died. In those days there were two cars: a large sedan and a large alterrain (230). Then, about one year ago, she was fired, along with all the others. Things changed after she left: Colette went away to teach (232); Conrad disappeared; Cob was planning to marry soon and close the house; but then Cob was murdered and Conrad returned (233).

Eight bedrooms on the second floor are Cob's room, Colette's room (previously mentioned (52)), and six guest rooms that were never used (235).

The trio hires Mrs. Peters to resume her job at Coldbrook mansion. Then they investigate for death records on both Coldbrook men.

Onomastics: For the cook Mrs. Keck (231), English name from

(Old Norse) personal name "Keikr" from Old West Scandinavian word "bent backwards"; or German nickname from Middle High German "Kec" (active, lively) which later changed its meaning to "Bold," "Forward," "Fresh." For the maid Ella-Jean (232), her name looks like "Elf Jean."

Economics: Mrs. Peters's weekly wage as Coldbrook housekeeper was 200 creds (236).

16. Him Again (241–56)

After Smithe leaves police headquarters, he realizes he is being followed. Smithe and Georges catch him, the little blond guy, who is Chick Bantz. He says he is employed by a government cop, Dane van Petten, who is the boyfriend of Colette.

Smithe tells Chick that Cob was murdered at the mansion a few weeks back (246). Smithe explains that he went to police headquarters to get public records. He shows the records to Chick.

Chick admits his job was to find out what Smithe was doing in New Delphi, who Smithe's two companions were, and how Smithe had found out that Dane and Colette were at the mansion (248).

They recruit Chick, and Smithe gives him the job to rent the local Arabella.

Smithe hears Mahala's report on seeing Colette examining people at the bus station (252). Georges thinks she was looking for Chick, but Smithe thinks it was Dane or "another that's better still" (254). (Who might Smithe be thinking of here? Perhaps the other sinister man, or the mysterious woman who had accompanied the two sinister men to Dr. Roglich's office.)

Onomastics: For Detective Serody, I find nothing. For Chick Bentz, "Chick" is an Anglo-Saxon name for one who struts like a rooster, and "Bantz" seems to be a variant of Bentz, "Little Bear," from "Dweller at the Sign of the Little Bear," or after Saint Benedictus, or for one who came from Benz in Germany. For Dane van Petten, "Dane" is "God is My Judge" (Daniel) or "From Denmark," and "van Petten" is a Dutch variant of Van Putten, meaning "from Putten," either the town Putten in Gelderland or the island Putten (sometimes merged into Voorne-Putten island) in South Holland. There is also "Van Petten," an unincorporated community in Illinois. (Note the similarity to "Coldbrook" in this regard.)

17. Escape (257–73)

Smithe takes a cab to the Coldbrook mansion, where Dane and Colette are.

Smithe's estimate that he has 15 more years of life is "stretching it" (261). He seems to have been at the library for three years, so it sounds like nine more years is more typical.

Colette and Dane clearly threaten Smithe (261).

Others arrive: first Mrs. Peters, then Chick and Arabella.

In private, Colette tells Smithe that she and Dane came looking for the trio because the trio sold emeralds (270).

Then Smithe shows her where he had hidden the book in the library, without telling her that it is currently hidden in the laboratory after he had retrieved it from the alien beach.

Frame Setting: "Have I described Arabella already?" (265)

Dynamic Shift: With Dane and Colette as a couple, Smithe is re-cast as Colette's pet. She tells Dane, "You have to get used to him and he has to get used to you, that's all. I love you, and he's very nice. He's useful, too, and loyal and clever. You should be glad I've got something like him" (263). Previously Smithe had identified with Puss in Boots, but now he fixes on the dog model, when he tells Arabella, "[W]e circle and snarl" (268). That is to say, he takes the role of Asta, the dog of Hammett's Nick and Nora in *The Thin Man*.

18. My Watch Struck Midnight (274–97)

Alone in the lab, Dane tells Smithe, "You're twenty years older than I am" (274), putting Smithe's visual age in the forties. Dane thinks that Conrad manufactured emeralds (275). Dane says the other sinister man was his boss (277). Smithe shows Dane the other world and locks him in.

Smithe then rigs the reactor to blow in a season or two.

Colette, unaware of Dane's disappearance, is spinning up dramatic new lifestyle changes: shuttering the mansion, buying a new house on the coast for herself and Mrs. Peters. All this to begin that evening by a group relocation to her apartment in Spice Grove.

She tells Smithe that Dane made her sign a confession.

Smithe finds Arabella in the library with a poem by another Smith. With her he flies to Taos Towers of Spice Grove. Then, when Arabella is asleep, he makes a deal with Colette, a blackmail to ensure that she will rent him from the library one day a year.

He outlines how Colette had killed her father Conrad, after Conrad had killed Cob.

Cob came in a cab (292; alluded to when Smithe came by cab (257)). Conrad strangled him.

Colette poisoned her father.

After getting this agreement, Smithe walks to the library to return himself.

The reactor that Smithe sabotaged blows up in January. Smithe writes the novel as further insurance policy.

Frame Tale: "I told you [the reader] yesterday" (274).

Cob's Humor: "[Conrad] had a sense of poetic fitness . . . greatly preferable to his son's sense of humor" (279). The humor referred to is probably in the vehicle names: the red convertible, almost certainly Cob's, is named "Geraldine" (which is an obscure color name for a shade of red); the yellow flitter is named "Canary" (a more obvious color name for a shade of yellow).

Flitter Flight: To Spice Grove from New Delphi mansion takes 45 minutes (285); specifically, to Taos Towers (286).

Hammett: Colette is revealed to be a lying schemer worse than Brigid O'Shaughnessy, the beautiful patron of Sam Spade in *The Maltese Falcon*. So in *A Borrowed Man* Wolfe crafts a Hammett medley, starting with the Continental Op (*Red Harvest*), adding a little Nick and Nora (*The Thin Man*), and ending with Sam Spade (*The Maltese Falcon*).

Puss in Boots: Like the cat hero, Smithe tricks the physically powerful monster.

Poe: The sealing of Dane into another world seems like the living entombment revenge in "A Cask of Amontillado" (1846), except here we can see the rationale for the sentence. The destruction of the Coldbrook family house and the ending of the Coldbrook family line has an echo to "The Fall of the House of Usher" (1839), which also has some living entombment to it.

Clark Ashton Smith: While Dane's one-way trip also matches the voyage in "The Door to Saturn," more importantly, in this final chapter Smith is mentioned by name and work, the poem beginning "Bow down . . ." being his poem "The Hashish Eater, or the Apocalypse of Evil" (1920). This 576-line epic has similarities to his aforementioned stories "The Door To Saturn" and "The Seven Geases" in providing a vivid tour through fantastic landscapes, this time different planets across a baroque universe. (In a correspondence to E. A. Smithe's experience, gems from other worlds appear in the poem: "Uranian sapphires fast in frozen blood, And amethysts from Mars.") Here are the opening six lines:

> Bow down: I am the emperor of dreams;
> I crown me with the million-coloured sun
> Of secret worlds incredible, and take
> Their trailing skies for vestment, when I soar,
> Throned on the mounting zenith, and illume
> The spaceward-flown horizons infinite.
> (collected in *Ebony and Crystal*, 1922)

The narrator begins full of his own power and glory, but in the midst of his tour a bit of discord shakes his equilibrium. The visions become tainted, hostile, and beyond his control. He begins a retreat, ultimately being driven to the edge of an abyss, where, overwhelmed, he is consumed by a frightful deity of supreme indifference. Here are the final lines:

> . . . but when I reach
> The verge, and seek through sun-defeating gloom
> To measure with my gaze the dread descent,
> I see a tiny star within the depths—
> A light that stays me, while the wings of doom
> Convene their thickening thousands: For the star
> Increases, taking to its hueless orb,

With all the speed of horror-changèd dreams,
The light as of a million million moons;
And floating up through gulfs and glooms eclipsed
It grows and grows, a huge white eyeless Face
That fills the void and fills the universe,
And bloats against the limits of the world
With lips of flame that open [. . .]

Commenting on the poem in his book *Clark Ashton Smith: Starmont Reader's Guide 49* (1990), Steven Behrends writes:

The judgment made against Man, and the *hubris* of man, is a negative one; at the same time, the tale told by the poem is extravagantly colorful and imaginative. In this way "The Hashish Eater" serves to encapsulate, as well as any other single work, the artistry and temperament of Clark Ashton Smith.(98)

E. A. Smithe's decision to destroy the portal to another world matches the endpoint of the poem "The Hashish Eater," in that it would be better for mankind to avoid embarking upon a tour of planets.

APPENDICES TO A BORROWED MAN

Appendix ABM1: Time, Mileage, and Money

Timeline

43 years ago: Coldbrook mansion built at New Delphi (51).

25 years ago (guess): Cob Coldbrook born.

23 years ago (guess): Colette Coldbrook born.

9 years ago (guess): Coldbrook family moves from New Delphi to Coldbrook mansion outside of New Delphi when Colette age 14 (52).

6 years ago: Jim Peters dies (228).

6 or 5 years ago: Nuclear plant installed at Coldbrook mansion (193).

5 years ago (guess): Coldbrook family portrait, with Colette in university skirt (56).

4 years ago: Mrs. Coldbrook dies (230); Conrad Coldbrook hires human staff for mansion (230). Colette age 19 (guess).

3 years ago: Colette at ruined garden in Spice Grove (24), presumably with Dane van Petten; E. A. Smithe arrives at Spice Grove Library.

1 year ago: Human staff at Coldbrook mansion is fired, replaced with robots in April (232); after which the red convertible is added to garage; and Colette moves to Spice Grove and begins teaching there.

January: Conrad goes away (six months ago).

July: Cob hires locksmith for safe, finds book and emeralds (289). Conrad returns, finds his safe looted, and kills Cob (295). Colette takes Cob's cash from emerald sales (295). Colette kills

Conrad (295).

July 20: Colette rents Smithe for ten days.

Next February?: reactor blows up mansion (288), more than two
quarters later (282); Smithe begins writing novel (288).

Murder Details

According to Colette, Conrad returns, screens Colette; Cob is at
Colette's apartment (291). Cob asks her to go and smooth things
over (291). She does so, but tells Cob to wait three or four days;
instead, Cob comes immediately by hovercab (291).

Colette poisons Conrad.

Other Details

Dane attaches to Colette regarding unpaid taxes on emeralds. He
makes her sign a confession about father's secret income, pressing
her about emeralds (280).

Dane learns about the book, either before Colette rents Smithe
or when she rents Smithe.

Smithe selling emeralds triggers Dane to take Colette to
mansion the next day? (270). Triggers Dane to order Chick to New
Delphi. Chick speaks to clerk at jeweler's (276).

Dane and his boss were the A-1 visitors (277).

Ten Days

0: July 20, Colette rents Smithe at 2 PM. Ruined garden. Taos
Towers. A-1 visitors at 11 PM.

1: July 21, Coldbrook mansion before lunchtime (55); hovercab
to Dr. Roglich at Owenbright. Owenbright hotel. Colette
snatched before dinnertime. Smithe walks to Owenbright
library.

2: July 22, Owenbright library breakfast. Meet Arabella of
Owenbright library. Visit by small blond man. Start of truck
trip 3 PM (102). Dinner after 7 PM.

3: July 23, Smithe buys blanket before breakfast. Library stop.
University library stop at lunchtime. Arabella of university
library on loan to Inspiration library. Colette and van Petten
from Owenbright to mansion at New Delphi.

4: July 24, Midmorning at Inspiration. Eight hours (five hours driving) from Inspiration to Spice Grove. Arrive near closing time.

5: July 25, Smithe checked out by officers Payne and Fish. He is taken to a safe house and questioned.

6: July 26, Escape after midnight. Bus 5 AM. Arrive at Spice Grove at night. Coldbrook mansion. Colette's scream.

7: July 27, Climb out window before breakfast. Smithe takes both Georges and Mahala to the jungle. Back on Earth, Smithe shows Georges the reactor. At 1 PM Georges picks the lock on the rental car. Then they sell the emeralds. Chick arrives in New Delphi, talks to a clerk at the jewelry store.

8: July 28, Before dawn, Smithe goes to the jungle, gets the rifle, has a run-in with monsters. Back on Earth, Smithe gets an eephone. The trio visits Mrs. Peters. Then they investigate death records. At lunchtime Smithe and Georges catch the blond man, Chick. Smithe takes cab to mansion; Colette and Dane are there, having come by her flitter (283). Mrs. Peters shows up (262). Chick brings Arabella from New Delphi library. Smithe locks Dane in the jungle world. Smithe accuses Colette of murder and makes a deal with her.

9: July 29, After midnight, Smithe starts the long walk from Taos Towers.

10: July 30

11: July 31, After midnight, Smithe arrives at Spice Grove library, overdue.

Internal Chronology of Composition

A Borrowed Man contains a few markers showing the passage of time in the frame tale.

The last two chapters were written sequentially over two days: "I think I told you [the reader] yesterday that the book was not really in Conrad Coldbrook's library anymore" (274) refers to information given in the previous chapter.

Smithe also indicates that he is writing after the mansion's reactor broke, which by other hints means it is in the first quarter of the next year, many months after his return to the library.

> Let me stop right here to say that I never have [told the authorities] and I never will. The reactor has gone up—it was on the news . . . I have been waiting for it, and now it has finally happened . . . So I am writing all this down, and I am going to hide it in the stacks. Someday somebody will find it there, but we will be dead and gone by then—or so I think. (288)

After writing this final chapter, it seems that Smithe wrote the first chapter, which is why it has "overture" elements to it: "I have been lying here on my shelf trying to figure out why I wrote all this" (9). He goes on, "I have been borrowed twice, thanks to all this about Colette, the locked doors, and my old book. Colette will come back next year and borrow me again. I have seen to it" (10).

The two borrowings were Colette last year and this year; a possible fakeout regarding his taking by the policemen Payne and Fish.

Having assigned the first chapter as being the last written, and noting the suggestion that each chapter was written in a day, one might assume that the second chapter was the first written. This is certainly possible, but there is also a chance that the first instance where Smithe describes the conditions of his writing (Chapter 9) marks the beginning of his writing.

Mileage

The text states that the direction from Spice Grove to New Delphi is southeast, and it seems to give two trips along this route, first with the route truck from Owenbright to Spice Grove and then with the hovercraft bus from Spice Grove to New Delphi. Putting together these two tracks, along with other, more speculative points like Taos Towers, gives a tentative list. Note that Smithe possibly has some glimmer of recognition for twenty-first century ruins out around Hapigarden.

- •Spice Grove
- •Taos Towers 165 miles from Spice Grove
- •Inspiration 280 miles from Spice Grove

- Rapid Rivers 385 miles from Spice Grove
- Hapigarden 495 miles from Spice Grove
- Owenbright
- Coldbrook House
- New Delphi
- Quinoafield

The Long Walk

If Taos Towers is 165 miles from Spice Grove and Smithe walks it in 48 hours, that is a staggering 83 miles per day. If it is only 110 miles, that is still a whopping 55 miles per day.

But Smithe has an eephone, and he has cash.

Money

Smithe's meal allowance 6 creds (102).
Mrs. Peters's weekly wage 200 creds (236).
Chick's cash gift to Smithe 300 creds (98).
Smithe's ten-day rental deposit 4,700 creds (16).
Hovercab sim's remaining buyout 34,000 creds (17).
Coldbrook house value 2,500,000 creds (69).

Appendix ABM2: *A Borrowed Man* as Mystery and/or Anti-Mystery

A Borrowed Man begins in the conventional way of a hardboiled mystery when a beautiful woman in danger hires the detective. Then come traditional set pieces involving dirty cops, bondage, rival dirty cops, and enhanced interrogation, but in this novel the lies and theories pile up so high that the story edges close to the "anti-mystery" found in such works as the Borges story "Death and the Compass" (1942) and the Eco novel *The Name of the Rose* (1980). I will show what I mean in analyzing five details: The Book and the Door, The Locksmith, The Death Reports, Colette's Changing Role, and Smithe's Motivation.

The Book and the Door

We are given so many details on the lock and how it works that it seems impossible that Cob found the book in the safe, since Conrad must have had it with him on the planet. If true, this means that Cob only found emeralds, and Colette is lying when she says Cob gave her the book. This leads Smithe to search for a second key, and his readers might suppose Smithe found the door unlocked on the jungle side the first time only because someone else had gone through less than two minutes before. Adding to this, Smithe thinks Colette was dragged screaming into a locked room, which implies the bad guys have a key.

But it turns out that bad guy Dane van Petten has no idea of the other planet; instead he believes that Conrad had manufactured the emeralds.

Therefore Conrad must have left the book in the safe and set the door to be unlocked on the jungle side. This was the best set up for him, as it would mean he was not reliant on having the book to return to Earth.

That would also mean that the loss of the book from the safe cut Conrad off from going back to the alien world.

The Locksmith

An interview with the locksmith who opened the safe for Cob seems like a very important lead to follow: he would say what was found in the safe, and the date he opened the safe. It never happens.

The Death Reports

The death reports bought from the police station would give such mundane yet critical information as date of deaths. These details are left out, presumably because they match the current timetable, but it seems like an affront, an anti-mystery twist, to avoid giving some positive data points as anchors amid the swirling blizzard of distracting details.

Colette's Changing Role

Colette is initially the damsel in distress, but in the end she is more of a co-conspirator.

That is, at the beginning she is "paranoid," fleeing from unknown forces.

When seen with Dane, she is instead a girlfriend with a sticky tax problem that her boyfriend is struggling to rectify.

If this is true, then the nude bondage session at Taos Towers was just a bit of pretend role-playing to scare Smithe into revealing the secret, or at least the book's location.

The faked abduction while Smithe was in the shower was presumably to see what Smithe would do. That Chick found Smithe at the Owenbright library shows that they had tracked him that far, but then they lost him as he was shipped out.

The enhanced interrogation was done by a different group, and as such it cannot be tallied toward Colette.

But Colette's lies pile up so high that one begins to wonder if she isn't actually a lot worse than a co-conspirator.

Her lies (a non-exhaustive list):

Her story that Cob got the lab keycard from the mortuary is a lie if Cob died first.

Colette tells Smithe that Conrad died about three weeks ago.

Colette tells Dr. Roglich that Conrad died six weeks ago.

Colette tells Smithe the lie about Merciful Maids.

Was the Owenbright "abduction" Colette's idea, or Dane's?

Was the "scream and go" maneuver Dane's idea, or Colette's?

These questions add additional "anti-mystery" tensions to the whole thing. Trying to figure out "what really happened" by cross-checking all of her stories seems a difficult task and a dubious strategy.

So we cut to the chase: In their last conversation, Smithe obliquely works through Colette's layers of lies until she says she saw Conrad strangle Cob. The truth might be worse than that: she may have set up the murder, and then lured Cob into the trap. Colette was resentful that Cob would get more inheritance as the first born, as a male (63), and as the one getting married (233), a detail which Colette never mentioned. So Cob had to die so she would inherit more, and then Conrad had to die so she would inherit sooner, but she knew nothing about the alien planet.

In any event, Colette seems much more malevolent than Hammett's Brigid O'Shaughnessy of *The Maltese Falcon*. Brigid is only a ruthless adventuress; Colette has killed her own father, and probably she set it up so that her father killed her brother as well.

Smithe's Motivation

While the anti-mystery tide rises, Smithe's own motivation develops stronger and sharper: he is literally fighting for his life.

Dane and Colette as a couple are threatening to kill him once he has solved the mystery for them. Colette makes a pretense of holding Dane back, but in reality, of course she will not: Smithe must die because he will know the illegal source of their fabulous emerald income.

Smithe threads the needle by eliminating Dane and defanging Colette with his blackmail deal.

Even with this, he knows Colette will kill him if given a chance, so months later he writes the novel *A Borrowed Man* and hides it in the library.

And, immediately after securing the deal with her, he starts walking to the library, even though it means walking for three days. Through this he mimics the way he inadvertently evaded them in his library truck ride.

Appendix ABM3: The Doctor of Fishbowl Mountain

In the 1970s, Gene Wolfe wrote a suite of stories involving "island," "doctor," and "death." The third, a novella titled "The Doctor of Death Island," collected in *The Island of Doctor Death and Other Stories and Other Stories* (1980), is the one where the protagonist Alan Alvard is a convict in prison for murder, with the unusual detail that he was given cryogenic suspension for decades, due to a disease, and resumes his life sentence after being revived and cured.

Before becoming a prisoner, Alvard had invented talking books, but he then murdered his business partner Barry Siegle. To gain freedom in the new era he finds himself in, Alvard tampers with a talking book in the prison library, thereby releasing characters from a Dickens anthology to wander freely into other books and documents, spreading beyond the prison walls through interlibrary loan, in a 1970s version of a hacker releasing a computer virus that only he can cure.

The novella has a theme of fictional characters mingling with the real world, such that at one point Alvard self-identifies as a bound text: "A book then. He was a book, of course . . . And this, this was a bookcase. This prison" (IODD, 266).

A Borrowed Man follows up on many details from the novella. In the novel, the library is like a prison for reclones, but worse, in that they are on death row, unlikely to live more than a dozen years. Like Alvard, all the reclones have been cast into the future. Like Alvard, Smithe gains temporary freedom from his prison through the use of a special book.

But the novella itself seems to have a curious history, perhaps tracing back to an unfinished novel. In a 1973 interview with Malcolm Edwards, Wolfe mentioned a stalled novel-in-progress called *In Grayhame Prison* (Wright's *Shadows of the New Sun,* p. 23). A few years later, "The Doctor of Death Island," the novella of Alvard in Grayhame Prison, first appeared in Dann's anthology *Immortal* (1978).

The shared name of the prison suggests a connection between the two projects, perhaps indicating that the novella is a reworking of the partial novel. Even though "The Doctor of Death Island" is the third in the "Archipelago" story sequence, there are hints that it comes from an earlier time in Wolfe's writing. On the downside, I feel it to be a lurch back into the style of *Operation ARES*. It is choppy, with Buck Rogers elements, along with a "mysteriousness" that seems counterproductive (I would compare the mystery of the seventh floor in "The Doctor of Death Island" to the lack of geographic footing in *Operation ARES*, even though the first has words and the second lacks words).

So *A Borrowed Man* seems to be a return to ideas Wolfe first sketched in "The Doctor of Death Island." This time the protagonist really is a created character trying to interact with the real world.

Appendix ABM4: "Civis Laputus Sum" and "The Eyeflash Miracles"

Two Gene Wolfe fictions with slight bearing on *A Borrowed Man* are "Civis Laputus Sum" and "The Eyeflash Miracles."

The short story "Civis Laputus Sum" (1975), collected in *Storeys from the Old Hotel,* is an early example in Wolfe's fiction where library books have been burned at the library, and this is conflated with people being burned. This notion finds full expression in *A Borrowed Man,* where the reclones face this same fate.

The story's narrator lives in a society that has voted to burn the fiction many years in the past. He has recently discovered this book, presumably the last survivor, "[I]n one of the incinerator bins, where it had wedged itself into a corner between the bin wall and the housing of the conveyor that would have fed it to the flames, and so survived these years. (Did you know you had escaped death so narrowly?)" (245). Later he recounts, "I went down into the Library basement . . . and found you, my book, and carried you away from the threat of dead fires" (249).

"The Eyeflash Miracles" (1976), collected in *The Island of Doctor Death and Other Stories and Other Stories,* is a novella set in a future America ruled from "Niagara," similar to the situation in *A Borrowed Man.* In contrast to Smithe's world, other familiar cities remain, including Martinsburg, Macon, Biloxi, Mobile, Pascagoula, Panama City, and Tallahassee.

The villain of the novella is a government agent from the Office of Biogenetic Improvement who uses the name "George Tib" and maybe "George Jefferson" (thus plural George, or "Georges") and he is tracking down a blind boy, for institutionalization if not execution; *A Borrowed Man* has an ex-cop, alias Georges Fevre, who is traveling with a mute woman who escaped institutionalization.

There is also a mixing of reality with fictitious characters, this time from L. Frank Baum's "Oz" books.

Appendix ABM5: Colette, the Coldest Coldbrook

Early on, Colette tells Smithe about the world population, "We're down to about one billion now. I'd halve that, if I could" (19).

For what it is worth, the world population of one billion was in AD 1804. The population of 500 million was at about AD 1600.

Colette seems to have had a hand in killing two of her relatives, half of her nuclear family.

Colette's mother was Joanne Rebecca Carole Coldbrook, daughter of Alice Carole. Joanne is shrouded in mystery.

Colette says of her mother, "She was [. . .] not social . . . other people, even people she knew and liked, stressed her out" (52).

Judy Peters, housekeeper, tells Smith, "She wasn't quite right, is what I heard, and that was the reason they'd never had servants. 'Bots would've been worse, I guess. They do pretty much whatever anybody tells them, is what I hear. But Mrs. C. wasn't exactly right sometimes, and I guess maybe she might have told one to kill her" (234).

Joanne seems to have followed the zero-population growth strategy of having only two children, Cob and Colette. Over time her increasingly reclusive nature led the family to relocate to the country mansion near New Delphi. Because of her suicidal nature, they did not have 'bots.

Joanne died four years ago (230). There are no details about her death. She may have committed suicide. Perhaps it was a "mercy killing" by Colette.

INTERLIBRARY LOAN

Edition cited: Tor (hb), ISBN 978-1-250-24236-5, 2020, 238 pp.

1. From the Spice Grove Public Library (7–23)
E. A. Smith begins with an overture, in the night time when all the thoughts come back to him.

The story starts when Smithe and fellow reclones Millie Baumgartner and Rose Romain are shipped out of Spice Grove together on interlibrary loan. The truck is much nicer than the one he rode in before. Millie is a middle-aged cookbook writer, Rose is a twenty-something romance writer. The season is winter.

The truck trip to Niagara is short, requiring only one night out, and they arrive the next day; but then they are switched to an old truck, and after three more nights of truck camping, they arrive at Polly's Cove on perhaps the fifth day (19). They meet librarian Prentice, who is deaf, and library volunteer Charlotte Lang. Smithe and Millie split up to explore while Rose bathes.

Proust: Because the overture is at night, it seems Proustian.

Onomastics: For Millie Baumgartner, "Millie" means "Industrious," and "Baumgartner" (German) means "Tree Gardner." For Rose Romain, "Rose" is the flower name, and "Romain" is the French form of "Roman." For Prentice, "Prentice" (Scottish/English) means "Apprentice." For Charlotte Lang, "Charlotte" is (French) "Strong" and "Vigorous," "Lang" is (Germanic) "Tall."

Geography: Smithe writes, "I've never been able to figure out where Saint Louis used to be" (13), which suggests some familiarity of his original with that city. Perhaps it ties in with his earlier note when he was "jouncing along in that truck and looking out at all that was left of one of the old cities where I used to live" (*A Borrowed Man,* 106). That is, he thought he saw the ruins of Saint Louis down around Owenbright.

More importantly for our own efforts at orientation, he mentions his belief that the mountains mentioned in *A Borrowed Man* are the Rockies. Further, he thinks Spice Grove is in former Nebraska, but it could be in the former Dakotas, "or even someplace up around [former] Winnipeg."

Commentary: The road trip to Niagara seems anomalously short compared with the other truck rides and bus rides Smithe has described. Even so, those other trips had many stops, and it turns out that from Winnipeg to Niagara Falls at 55 mph it takes 20 hours, which sounds about right. Not an anomaly.

Anomalies: Initially the fact that librarian Prentice is deaf seems at odds with the society of the times, given that Mahala's muteness is cause for being institutionalized in *A Borrowed Man.* Then again, Prentice can read lips, and she can speak, which might be the necessary distinction.

Economics: The price of three warm coats was twice what Smithe had in creds from Colette, so he bought three blankets, which left a little over (19).

Wolfeana: The iron spiral staircase in the library, and the view from the library, recall "The Fifth Head of Cerberus" (1972), where the library of Port Mimizon has a wide spiral stair (in the style of The Guggenheim Museum in New York City), and the narrator, from the top of the library, looks out upon the landscape and sees, "To the south, the masts of the ships in the harbor" (*The Fifth Head of Cerberus,* 9).

2. What the Shirt Showed (24–28)

Upon meeting up again, Millie tells Smithe about a young library patron named Chandra with whom she spoke. But Millie also says she saw a little girl in a white dress, a person who melted into a wall (26–27).

Smithe notices his new used shirt has bloodstains that washing failed to remove.

Anomalies: Millie, talking about patron Chandra, seems to be talking about pheasant-cooking Charlotte (26). Probably just a natural slip by the character.

Onomastics: "Chandra" is Hindi for "the Moon." The English pronunciation is SHAN-dra; while the Hindi pronunciation is CHUN-dra.

Hammett: Ghost sighting is a hint of the supernatural, which lines up with *The Dain Curse* (1929), the Continental Op's singular spooky case. The curse in question causes violent and sudden death upon those near to Dain women.

3. The House on Signal Hill (29–43)

On the third day, Smithe is checked out by Chandra for her mother. On the walk to her house, Chandra asks for secret sweets, and Smithe agrees to provide one in exchange for information. Chandra tells him her mother is haunted by magical assassins, possibly due to an accident on a boat years before. Chandra has seen a weird talking dog come into her mother's bedroom at night a number of times (35).

Smithe suspects the mother is a paranoid schizophrenic and has infected the child with these delusions.

He meets the woman, Adah Fevre, who asks him to examine a book of hers. It contains a map pasted in on the inside back cover. She has him touch a possibly drugged spot on the map, and when he does, he has a strange vision (40).

Mrs. Fevre tells him she had already tried a Smithe copy to solve this mystery (42). She returned that copy in order to rent him.

Typo: "Charlotte wanted to know" (32) should be "Chandra." Because Smithe is still learning to work on a screen, and there are two names beginning "CHA," there is a possibility that this typo might be an autofill error from his typing or his speaking.

Anomalies: Smithe says, "We got here yesterday" (37), but it was the third day. He might be just being conversationally vague.

Onomastics: "Adah" is a Hebrew name meaning "Ornament," and it is also an Urdu name meaning "Adornment."

Echo Chamber: Like *A Borrowed Man*, this mystery starts with a book that is somehow a key. The location, a house on the coast, is what Colette was aiming for at the end of *A Borrowed Man;* the situation at the house, with a sickly, isolated mother and her teenage daughter, replays the history of Colette's youth. The name "Fevre" returns, this time as an authentic surname rather than an alias. Again, there is an island.

Mystery of the Bookplate: Smithe says, "I did [look at the bookplate in front], and I felt certain it wasn't yours. Was I mistaken?" To which she answers, "No. Someday I must remember to ask you what made you so confident. My name is Adah Fevre" (38).

Mystery of the Book: Smithe asks if Barry got the name "Chandra" from the book (43).

Clark Ashton Smith: In touching the spot on the map, Smithe has a vision: "I stood among a dark throng of phantom figures: a half-starved girl whose lips could not quite conceal her teeth, a leering potbellied old man, a hairy dwarf who shook three spiked balls at the end of a staff, and many more" (40). This lurid tableau seems like something from Clark Ashton Smith, but the poem "The Hashish Eater" bears no direct traces.

Doubling: An older copy of Smithe.

4. Adah's Story (44–56)

Adah's mother wanted her to marry a doctor. She rebelled but it happened anyway. Barry Fevre and his brother Simon taught at the university in Spice Grove. Smithe correctly guesses that Adah grew up in High Plains, which seems to upset Adah.

Adah and Barry got married. In the third year, she became pregnant and Barry had a sabbatical year. She forced him to take her along on his mysterious trip, deep down sensing that he was looking for cadavers, a necessary resource for his medical classes.

Her guess was right. He hired a boat, a fishing vessel named the *Third Sister.* Often at night, the boat woke Barry to examine something in the water, and one night, Barry did not come back, having gotten onto another boat. Before leaving, Barry told the boat to return to Polly's Cove.

Adah returned to Polly's Cove, had baby Chandra, and continues waiting for Barry's return.

Adah's Cop Suitor: Adah mentions that before marrying she went out with "all kinds of men," including a policeman who "married somebody else" (44). A page later, when Smithe guesses Adah grew up in High Plains (45), we do not know the clue or clues that led him to this, for example, an accent or phrase that marks a person as being from High Plains. The only thing we know about High Plains from *A Borrowed Man* is that George Franklin was previously a policeman there, and he had a wife at that time. This seems like a tenuous link, that George was Adah's cop boyfriend. Since the name "Fevre" is relatively rare, as established by Smithe in *A Borrowed Man,* then hypothetically George Franklin would make his alias "Fevre" from his old girlfriend's name, but Fevre is her married name, not her maiden name, which greatly complicates things.

Perhaps it ties in with the mystery of the bookplate: maybe the name in the book is George Franklin. When Smithe says he felt certain it was not Adah's (38), he would thus be inviting her to say how she had gotten it, perhaps from a relative, living or deceased, with that fairly common name. She dodges the question, because she claims to have found the book in Barry's luggage after he disappeared (43), but then when she talks about the policeman who subsequently married someone else, that detail adds more weight to his hunch.

By Adah's account, she was previously a great reader (45). A serious suitor would give her a book. A very serious suitor would give her a book dear to himself.

Wolfeana: The "fifth suitor wins the bride" is a trope in *Peace* (1975) and in the field hospital romance of *The Citadel of the Autarch* (1983).

Doubles: Barry Fevre has a brother, probably also a Dr. Fevre.

Onomastics: "Barry" (from Gaelic) means "Fair-Headed" or "Fair-Haired." "Simon" (from Hebrew) means "Listen" or "Hearing," but there is another line of association ("Reed-like," "Wavering," or "Sand-like") which probably derives from the cruel and vengeful behavior of the first Simeon (Genesis 49: 5–7).

Bible: There are a number of Simons in the New Testament, including Simon Peter (Saint Peter), Simon the brother of Jesus, and Simon the Cyrenian who carried the cross of Jesus for a time on the walk to the crucifixion.

Rhymes for Crimes: Smithe's remembered verse about Burke and Hare is an authentic rhyme of the place and time. It is interesting that graverobbing had become so difficult in Edinburgh that the two friends turned to murder to obtain cadavers for sale.

All this talk of Burke and Hare by Adah casts a shady suggestion about cadaver-hunting brothers Barry and Simon Fevre.

Anomalies: Adah says she sold their house in High Plains and received a lot of money for it, since "Homes are so costly there" (56). Smithe says, "Because of the university, I suppose." The university discussed before was in Spice Grove. Smithe might be suggesting that the house was in Spice Grove, too, and her memory is slipping here.

Adah repeatedly refers to the ship as the *Third Sister,* but the name seems to be the *Three Sisters,* as Smithe mentioned in the opening of Chapter 1. Presumably this is a sign of her weak memory.

5. A Cold Tea Party (57–78)

Smithe and Chandra go to the kitchen. Smithe detects that Mrs. Heuse, the cook, is a reclone. Her secret is that she is overdue, claimed lost for nearly two years.

Smithe suspects Mrs. Heuse is somehow behind the ghostly dog, perhaps that she herself is Adah's dog, or Adah has forgotten she has a dog (60). He walks back to the public library where he confirms Elizabeth Heuse was a cookbook author. Millie catches up with him, tells how Heuse was an animal lover and Millie once saw her traumatized by a question on roasting dog (61).

Smithe compares the map in the book with the treasure map in the novel *Treasure Island* (63). He compares his separate loyalties to Chandra and to Adah.

Smithe wants to talk to his old copy. He has Millie run interference with the librarian. He finds the other Smithe dead with a slashed throat (67). He fears it may have been suicide.

Dr. Fevre checks out Rose and Millie (69).

Back at the house, Smithe talks with Chandra about her father (73). The timeline gets squirrelly, and Smithe asks if she was with them on the boat. No, she was in High Plains with Aunt Laura, who is her father's little sister (75).

Smithe proposes that Barry requested Rose and Millie be loaned to Polly's Cove in order to prevent someone in Spice Grove from seeing him with them (77).

Smithe theorizes that Dr. Fevre has learned about Mrs. Heuse, a cheap way to get a skilled slave (78). Perhaps Mrs. Snow, the housekeeper, told him.

Anomalies: Smithe says of the older Smithe copy, "Me in another forty years" (65), but this gives a much longer lifespan for reclones than the range he gave before, which was around a dozen years.

Hammett: The mysterious death of the older Smithe (67) fits the pattern of the Dain Curse, being the violent and sudden death of people close to Dain women.

Treasure Island: The famous 1883 adventure novel by Robert Louis Stevenson is about pirates, buried treasure, and shifting alliances. Smithe mentions Jim Hawkins by name, paired with Long John Silver (63), and it seems likely he sees himself as the boy-hero Jim. He must also be wondering who will be his "Long John Silver," which is a complex question since the pirate has different personas (an easy-going sea cook called "Barbeque"; a cold and cunning pirate called "Long John Silver"), and in the course of the novel the boy and the pirate are on different sides, sometimes allied, at other times in opposition.

Onomastics: For cook Elizabeth Heuse, "Elizabeth" (Hebrew) "God is My Abundance," and "Heuse" (German) meaning "Lively" or "Fresh" (showing some similarity to cook Keck in A Borrowed Man, whose name also can mean "Lively" or "Fresh"). For Mrs.

Snow, the surname "Snow" (English) has nothing to do with snow, but "White Haired" or "Very Pale Complexion." For Laura Fevre, "Laura" is a plant name, from the bay laurel, which, in the Greco-Roman world of antiquity, was made into laurels awarded for victory, honor, or fame. For Jim Hawkins, "Hawkins" means "Little Hawk."

6. From Library Custody (79–92)

After a great deal of research, Smithe talks with Laura Fevre, aunt of Chandra. She tells him that Barry is on sabbatical again, seven years after the last one. Laura thinks he is getting more cadavers and directs Smithe to Peggy, the doctor's assistant. This turns out to be Professor Margaret Pepper. Smithe tricks her into giving the name of the island Lichholm (82). She claims Barry does not have a flitter.

Adah bursts in to organize the expedition. She claims pirate heritage from Morgan, on her mother's side.

Smithe privately wonders who will feed the dog but supposes Mrs. Heuse will (84).

Smithe goes to the public library for dinner to examine the other reclones for possible recruitment. There is Nigel Hart, a military historian, and Hans von Rhein, who wrote on horology, but the most promising is Audrey Hopkins, a sailing expert.

Smithe sleeps at the library and sits next to Audrey at breakfast. Hoping to recruit her, he mentions the ambiguity of time since Barry left Adah, which she reports as being seven years or twelve years (88).

Audrey agrees to join the expedition, and Smithe gets her checked out. Smithe mentions his suspicion that Barry has more than two houses (89). They locate and inspect the *Three Sisters*.

Audrey points out "Lichholm" means "Isle of Corpses" (92).

Onomastics: For Margaret Pepper, "Margaret" means "Pearl," and "Pepper" is an occupational name for one who deals in spices. For Nigel Hart, "Nigel" is "Champion" or "Black"; and "Hart" is a male deer. For Hans von Rhein, "Hans" is "God is Gracious," and "von Rhein" is "From the River Rhein" (and "horology," his subject of specialty, is the study of the measurement of time; also applied to the art of making clocks and watches).

For Audrey Hopkins, "Audrey" means "Noble Strength," and English/Welsh/Irish "Hopkins" means "Son of Hob" (where "Hob" is a form of "Robert," meaning "Renowned Fame").

Sea Song: When Audrey sings "We did seal, We did seal . . ." (88), it is from the folk song "Davy Lowston," a ballad about sealers abandoned in New Zeeland in 1810. After nearly four years of great deprivation, they were rescued by the *Governor Bligh*.

Bulgakov: The Soviet author's posthumous novel *The Master and Margarita* (1967) is modeled on Faust and his assistant Gretchen. Wolfe mentioned Bulgakov in a list of authors he admired (Wright's *Shadows of the New Sun,* p. 27), and traces of *The Master and Margarita* show up in Wolfe's work. That Dr. Fevre's assistant is named Margaret seems an important allusion.

Pirate Morgan: Sir Henry Morgan (1635–1688) was a Welsh privateer, arguably the best-known pirate, and model for much pirate fiction. He was married, but the couple had no children, so his estate passed to his nephews, the children of his brother-in-law.

Treasure Island: Adah claiming pirate heritage certainly puts her into contention for being Smithe's Long John Silver, and the fact that she has a passive persona and a manic persona adds a bit to it.

Economics: The ship rental is 1,000 creds to begin, then 300 when they sailed out, followed by 100 for every day after the first week (90).

Commentary: Smithe never mentions how he came to know that the vessel referred to by Adah as the *Third Sister* was actually the *Three Sisters,* but he is using the latter at the beginning of Chapter 6.

7. Conversations (93–107)

The expedition sets out, the members going through seasickness. Smithe confronts Adah about damaging reclones like his older edition. She admits the older Smithe had said Barry was unfaithful to her (96).

They meet the other ship in a rough sea and Barry Fevre comes aboard.

Commentary: That the older Smithe told Adah that Barry was unfaithful suggests that the reclone had gone to Spice Grove where he saw Barry cavorting. This ties in with the earlier idea that Barry did not want someone in Spice Grove to see him with Rose and Millie (77).

Imitation Life Imitates Art: Smithe refers to his original as "the manuscript" (99).

Geography: Mention of Port Purity (101).

Anomalies: Together on the top deck, Audrey and Smithe spot a ship with sails, and she tells him something about that type of vessel (102). He goes down to the bridge to get a better view of it, and the AI says it is a lugger, and shows him a better view. When he gets back up on the top deck, Audrey says she had not seen it until their ship turned toward it (104). This seems like a strange splice. Or there were two boats, and the *Three Sisters* showed Smithe the one that was more interesting to the ship.

8. To Lichholm (108–19)

Smithe wrestles with his theories about Dr. Fevre and the dead older Smithe reclone. The older Smithe must have found something about Barry. Reporting on this had given him a mutilation, but this same cut, along with a return to the library, meant the reclone was no longer a danger to Barry.

Barry talks to Chandra, explaining that Adah has an emotional disorder, and that this is the reason for his absence. He tells them all about the island. Smithe asks about the treasure, but the doctor is silent on that topic (114). Smithe seems to guess that it was Barry who drew the treasure map.

In private, Smithe and Audrey go through theories, one being that Barry came to their ship expecting Prof. Peggy Pepper was there (116).

In the later afternoon they sight Lichholm (118).

9. The Only Village on Corpse Island (120–35)

They arrive at the harbor the next day. Barry is boarding with a family, and he finds another house, with the old Eiriksdatter couple, for Adah, Chandra, Audrey, and Smithe.

After dinner, Smithe and Audrey talk over the logistics of Barry's movement and behavior. On their side, they took about a week of prep time before setting out, then three days of travel before sighting the lugger (122–23). Smithe figures that Mille and Rose were on the lugger with Barry (124).

So Smithe and Audrey walk over to that house where Barry is staying and there they find the two reclones, just as suspected. Furthermore, it becomes clear that the doctor had checked out Millie to be a cook slave and Rose to be a sex slave. Millie confirms it, noting that Barry had established the pattern in Spice Grove, which is why he had requested them through interlibrary loan.

Smithe privately asks Millie if Barry had slashed the old Smithe's throat on the way out the Spice Grove Public Library door. She denies it.

Smithe theorizes that Adah wanted a Smithe from Spice Grove because such a library resource might know any university faculty gossip about Barry. Millie will not talk about the faculty gossip at this time.

On the walk back to their place, Smithe and Audrey banter about the old holidays. She shares her daydreams.

Onomastics: For Eiriksdatter, this is "Eric's Daughter." "Eirik" is Norwegian, the younger form of (Old Norse) "Eiríkr," meaning "Eternal Ruler."

Typo: "Polly's Grove" (127) should be "Polly's Cove."

Anomalies: The banter between Smithe and Audrey about Christmas and Halloween causes calendar consternation. Audrey sings "Silent Night." Smithe says she is rushing it, saying "It must be almost a quarter year away" (132). She counters with a joke about the next day being Christmas, and he corrects her by saying it will be Halloween.

This is all the more puzzling because the novel began in winter

(12), with snow.

Technically, winter does not start until just a few days before Christmas, but often enough people equate snow with winter. The quarter is a three-month unit.

Then again, Smithe might just be joking with her: Their shared discussion is how old-timers like themselves remember Halloween, Thanksgiving, and Christmas. So the joke might be that they both know the current date is nearly Thanksgiving, but she is singing a Christmas song, so he is exaggerating by saying it is the night before Halloween. Thematically it is important to note the Halloween spookiness of preparing to enter a vast frozen necropolis.

10. The Cottage in the Cavern (136–52)

In the morning, five ride a sleigh to the cave: Barry, Adah, Chandra, Audrey, and Smithe. Chandra tells them her father has won the confidence of the villagers through his free medical treatment.

Smithe believes that in entering the cave he is in the spot marked on the treasure map (140).

After they pass through many chambers, Audrey sees a body that looks like her and she examines it with Smithe (143). They are interrupted by a stranger, a tall man bearing a flat green box. They abruptly realize they are separated from the group. The man pushes his metal box into Smithe's hands, but when Smithe turns it sideways, reality shifts into jungle, sliding back into ice when he turns it level again. After this, Audrey says she feels dizzy (144).

After a while they encounter Prof. Peggy Pepper, who is also looking for Barry. The tall man calls himself Sven. Peggy identifies all three as reclones. Together they search for Barry.

Surprisingly, Peggy tells Smithe how she came to belief in the soul after dissecting many cadavers (149).

Smithe hands the box to Audrey and goes down a scree. Halfway down he loses his light and sits down to rest a bit, but suddenly Chandra finds him. She leads him to a house in the vast cavern.

Imitation Life Imitates Art: Prof. Peggy Pepper's tag of Sven as a reclone is questionable. Presumably she is basing her assessment upon such details as the non-symmetry of Sven's face.

Anomalies: That Chandra knows about her father's use of free medical treatment to win over the islanders seems a little odd, seeing as how she has not seen him for most of her life, and she has never been to the island. Then again, this nugget is exactly the sort of thing he might have told her during the transit time to the island on the *Three Sisters.*

When Smithe writes, "The cave kept getting bigger . . . by jumps" (141–42), it hints at the cave having gates between worlds, except that there is no nausea at the transitions.

When Smithe is found by Chandra, her sudden arrival hints that he might have fallen asleep or died.

11. Jingle Bells (153–63)

The cottage is made of ice blocks. Inside is Adah, Barry, Sven, and two "angels." Smithe berates the couple, and Adah moves to strike him with an axe, but Sven halts the axe at the top of its swing. Barry sends Chandra to find Audrey.

The "angels" Ricci and Idona are two young women revived by Barry. Adah says he has a harem.

An hour later, Chandra brings Peggy and Audrey. Audrey gives the green box back to Smithe.

Smithe had pulled the map out of the book and has it with him.

Wolfeana: The halting of an axe at the top of its swing is a trick used by Severian in the first chapter of *The Shadow of the Torturer* (1980). The idea of young women being revived at a necropolis seems hauntingly familiar, too.

The Doctor of Death Island: Cryogenic revival is here being discovered by Barry, the doctor of Cadaver Island; in "The Doctor of Death Island," Alvard uses an already established cryogenic suspension to travel into the future.

Puns: When Adah snaps, "He has a harem. The inmates are dead" (156), she effectively recasts "Isle of Corpses" as "I love corpses."

Clark Ashton Smith: Necrophilia is a recurring theme in the writings of Clark Ashton Smith. In the sixteen Zothique stories alone, five feature necrophilia ("The Empire of the Necromancers" (1932), "The Charnel God" (1934), "Necromancy in Naat" (1936), "The Death of Ilalotha" (1937), and "Morthylla" (1953)). That is about one in three. In addition, there is the play set in Zothique, "The Dead Will Cuckhold You" (1951). Wolfe explores this in his Zothique-anthology story, "A Traveler in Desert Lands" (1999), collected in *Innocents Aboard.*

Anomalies: Barry claims that Chandra knows the ice caves better than he does (156). Supposedly this is Chandra's first time to visit the place, so it seems like a strange splice. Then again, during the same father-daughter time on the *Three Sisters* when Barry might have told Chandra about his free clinic for the fisher folk, perhaps he showed her a non-magical map of the cave interior, and she studied it with fervor.

Commentary: The surprise that Smithe has the magical treasure map on his person might explain why Sven gave him the box.

12. Something You Do On a Boat (164–68)

Prof. Peggy Pepper's flitter seats four, and takes the four fully humans back. The other six ride in the boat with a cargo of cadavers.

In talking, Rose says Barry was worried Idona would stick her knife in him.

Onomastics: Ricci is (Norse) "Forever Strong." Idona is (Norse) "Active in Love," which ties in with "Idona wanted to talk about sex, and did . . ." (165).

Economics: When Smithe signed the boat over to Barry, Smithe "pocketed the refund" (166). Would that be all 1,300 creds?

Comment: Idona is another murderously jealous type, like Adah.

It is curious that Prof. Pepper knew Barry did not have a flitter, yet she seems to have one herself. Almost an anomaly, but not quite.

13. The Cheap Detective (169–79)

They arrive at Polly's Cove almost a week later than Prof. Peggy and the Fevres. After a while, Chandra checks out Audrey again. Smithe thinks on writing this adventure, and how the old Smithe must have killed himself, but after another while, Chandra rents him because her father Barry is dead.

Audrey had found the body on Friday before supper; Chandra got Smithe there three full days plus a few hours later (implying it is Monday). Barry had been shot in the neck with a big arrow. There are eight suspects in the house, all women.

Smithe hears the sound of high heels walking upstairs (176). Chandra suspects Rose or Idona of murdering Barry.

That night, Smithe and Audrey sleep next to Chandra's bed and Smithe awakens to an intruder in the darkness, a big humanoid who goes out the door and disappears. It seems he took the murder weapon, the big arrow, with him (179).

Smithe's Original: Reference to "Shasta the Cougar" points to the University of Houston mascot; to which we add Smithe's previous mention of Saint Louis. The suggestion seems to be that the Smithe "manuscript" attended the University of Houston and lived in Saint Louis for a considerable time before and/or after university.

Uncertain Echoes: The sound of high heels walking upstairs (176) seems related to the overture's mention of Chandra's Mary Janes (8), except that Mary Janes are not high heels, and, more importantly, Chandra is with Smithe when they hear the sound. Of the eight other women (Adah, Audrey, the cook Mrs. Heuse, Idona, Millie, Ricci, Rose, and the unseen housekeeper Mrs. Snow), the younger women, Idona, Ricci, and Rose, seem most likely to be wearing high heels.

Anomalies: Smithe asks Chandra, "Your parents didn't return Audrey to the library?" (174) when he had already known the details on that (169).

When Smithe counts out eight suspects (175), he is including Chandra, but forgetting Mrs. Snow.

The text suggests that Smithe sits twice, which seems a strange splice.

About the sitting, granted that Smithe calls the brocade chair "my chair," and he runs his fingers on its armrest, but it seems he might be doing this while standing. Maybe not, maybe an armrest is so low down that it would be faintly ridiculous to lean over and stroke it. Then again, the text has established he is eager to sit, so maybe he is miming to encourage young Chandra to invite him to sit. When she does finally sit, her furniture choice forces his choice of where to sit, and he thankfully takes the wingback chair to better face her.

The text suggests that Smithe enters the house twice, which seems a strange splice. But for me, there is the vexing lack of detail about the murder scene—I find no hint whatsoever.

Where was the body found? Smithe suggests that it would be hard for any of the women to use such a bow (175), but the big arrow could have been used as a handheld stabbing weapon (177). Was there a trail of blood showing that Barry had crawled to there from another place? Does the location of the body allow for the arrow to have been shot, or to have been used as a stabbing weapon?

So with all that, I half wonder if the second entry into the house is actually at the back door after looking around at the backyard, or something like that, an activity which goes without comment because there is nothing gained from it. (Granted, it could also be a strange splice, like spotting the ship with Audrey, then coming back and she seems to spot it for the first time.)

14. Of the Continental Police (180–87)

Backing up in the timeline to the beginning of this murder mystery: on the first day, Smithe interviews the women. Adah says somebody is trying to take her house away from her; Ricci says the house is haunted.

At midnight, Chandra yells there is somebody under her bed, but Smithe finds nobody.

The next night is when the intruder comes in, a man wearing

a helmet with feathers (183). Smithe grabs for him and gets a big knife. He hides the knife at the library.

Smithe is overdue so he goes back to the library, as does Audrey. A few days later a man checks out Audrey for two weeks, and Smithe is tempted to use the big knife on him. A week later a female cop named Katrine Turner checks out Smithe. She wants his help in solving the case of Barry's murder.

Anomalies: Still no glimpse of the murder scene. Smithe mentions that a bow is quiet when fired (182) and could have been shot through an open window (182). Did the murder site have an open window, in winter? This is definitely anti-mystery.

In this version of the encounter with the intruder, Smithe reaches for the intruder and dislodges a big knife (183); in the earlier version, he did not try to even sit up until after the intruder left the room (178). It might be explained as a narrative streamlining, followed by a correction. But the two versions seem so different that it feels more like a strange splice.

15. Strangers in the House (188–94)
Officer Turner takes him by groundcar to a compound where he is questioned for six or seven hours.

On their drive back to town, Smithe tells her about the midnight intruder and the dozen locked doors. They go to the house and break through the locked door that had been installed by the other side. The portal leads to a weird treehouse at the top of a very tall tree.

Despite Smithe's fierce resistance, they begin the manhunt.

Onomastics: For Katrine Turner, "Katrine" is the Scandinavian form of Catherine, meaning "Pure," and "Turner" is an occupational name for "One Who Works a Lathe."

Anomalies: Turner says she is "supposed to bring you back to the house where I picked you up" (188–89), but she had gotten him at the public library (184), which he had subsequently referred to (186). This is a strange splice, unless a puny public library seems like a "house" when compared to vast concrete compounds.

The first view of the treehouse shows "no windows" (192), but after one step inside, he goes over to a window (192–93). Then again, portals are not necessarily flush with a wall at both ends, since the jungle door was free-standing among the trees.

16. Among the Leaves (195–202)

Smithe continues wrestling with his options regarding Officer Turner as they work their way down the stairway inside the hollow tree. They find a door onto a path, but the "path" is really a branch that Turner falls off, leaving him with the pistol.

He practices with the pistol, then climbs down the outer bark. Turner is unharmed by her fall, so he returns the pistol to her and they continue their manhunt.

The smaller plants they move among are very strange, having spooky, animal-like attributes.

At night Smithe dreams a dream he is back at Alice's Tea Room.

When he wakes up, he sees they have been found by their suspect, the man with the feathered helmet. The suspect tries to tie them up but they kill him.

Turner declares the case resolved and they go back to Earth.

Web of Worlds: The situation of portals to worlds seems like the Kuttner and Moore series beginning with *The Dark World* (1946), crossed with the H. Beam Piper "Paratime" series of interdimensional police work, tracking crimes across the worlds.

Wolfeana: When Smithe uses a trigger-block maneuver on Officer Turner on the branch path (196), he echoes Incus using that trick on the airship in *Exodus from the Long Sun* ("My Defense," 373).

Edgar Rice Burroughs: The path that is a tree limb, and the action there upon, evoke a scene from *Pirates of Venus* (1932), wherein the Earthman Carson Napier, on his first outing in the very high limb path of the trees, is with his Venusian friend Kamlol when they are attacked by a giant spider: "The footing was secure enough for Kamlol and the spider, for they were both accustomed to it, but to me it seemed very precarious. Of course the tree limbs were enormous and often the branches were laced together, yet I felt anything but secure." The monster disables the

Venusian and pounces upon the hero:

> As it crashed upon me, my body toppled from the great branch upon which I had been standing, and I felt myself falling. Fortunately, the interlacing, smaller branches gave me some support; I caught at them and checked my fall, bringing up upon a broad, flat limb ten or fifteen feet below. I had clung to my sword, and being unhurt, clambered back as quickly as I could to save Kamlot from further attack. (*Pirates of Venus*, Chapter 6)

Alice in Wonderland: The plant-animals are weird in a creepy, Wonderland way, which might be why Smithe later dreams of Alice's Tea Room.

Clark Ashton Smith: A bit from the poem "The Hashish Eater," whose opening Arabella had read in *A Borrowed Man*, here gives us some freakish plants:

> I see a host of naked giants, armed
> With horns of behemoth and unicorn,
> Who wander, blinded by the clinging spells
> Of hostile wizardry, and stagger on
> To forests where the very leaves have eyes
> (*Ebony and Crystal*, 1922)

Just like in the poem, Smithe sees leaves with eyes.

Commentary: It is possible that Turner is the third police officer, the unidentified woman who was with Dane van Petten and his boss in *A Borrowed Man* when they visited Dr. Roglich (as reported in *A Borrowed Man* Chapter 6).

Alice K. Turner: The officer's name is Katrine Turner. While camping with her, Smithe dreams of Alice's Tea Room, which might suggest a linkage between "Alice" and officer "K. Turner." Alice K. Turner's middle name is not widely known; it was "Kennedy."

17. Shelf Life Resumed (203–206)

At the house, Smithe explains he is overdue. Eventually Chandra is sent with him to the public library to return him and collect the deposit.

At the library he asks after Rose and Millie, pointing out that their patron Barry had died. Librarian Prentice questions Smithe and puts him on the case to assist volunteer Charlotte Lang in retrieving the two reclones. He awaits her rental of him.

Anomalies: While Smithe is at Adah's house due to Officer Turner, there should be no deposit for Chandra to collect (203). This detail seems like a strange splice of when Chandra had returned him before; and it comes after Smithe has been waxing nostalgic: "Every step we took was rerunning a part of my life that I remembered much too vividly, running my life backward."

Commentary: Smithe is misleading Prentice, perhaps so that Rose and Millie might get some kind of freedom. As slaves.

18. Buck Baston (207–212)

Buck Baston, a reclone of a Western genre author, stops at Smithe's shelf at 9:45 AM to recruit him for Ms. Harper Heath.

The job is a haunted house. Buck thinks the "haunts" came because of Ricci. Barry's "angel" Ricci was bought by Ms. Heath from Barry's estate after Barry's murder. Ricci is the one who asked for Smithe. Ms. Heath checked out Buck a week ago, and is now renewing him.

Ms. Heath checks out Smithe and questions him as they fly in her silver flitter.

Onomastics: For Buck Baston, "Buck" of course means "Male Deer" (it also ties in with the "Buck Rogers" thread), and "Baston" might be (Old French) "Beadle" or "Verger" for a person of authority, or (Old English) "Inhabitant of Bak's Farmstead." The "beadle" angle connects with the surname of reclone Johnston Biddle (in *A Borrowed Man,* Chapter 7).

Smithe says his name "Ern" means "eagle" (208). It is a type of eagle in Europe and Greenland, which is especially poignant as an eagle pairing with Arabella as "Eagle Heroine." It also shares a bird of prey connection with Jim Hawkins ("Little Hawk"), the boy-hero of *Treasure Island.*

For Harper Heath, "Harper" is an occupational name for one who plays a harp, and "Heath" is a locational name for one who lives on or near a moor or heath.

For Barry F. Fevre (210), the middle initial is a surprise. How much mischief? If "F" is for "Franklin," that is a lot of mischief.

Echo Chamber: The haunted house motif comes up again. This time, it seems the ghosts came in the wake of a young woman, Ricci; which echoes back to the girl in the white dress at the Polly's Cove library who seems to have come in the wake of a girl, Chandra. Perhaps Chandra and Ricci are some kind of unintentional spirit mediums who are always "on."

Wolfeana: The massive dictionary in the library lobby, that Buck says, "Takes two jest to turn a page" (209), sounds like a certain massive "coffee table" art book from *Bibliomen* (1984), beginning with "Bernard A. French."

An unintentional spirit medium who is always "on" is an apt description for Wolfe's character Latro, whose adventure begins in *Soldier of the Mist* (1986).

19. At Home with the Heaths (213–22)

From the air, Ms. Heath shows the growing, living house. She mentions Venice, Italy, so that place seems to still exist.

On the ground, Baston says the house grows two little rooms or one big room per day.

Smithe finds a room to wait for ghosts after sunset. He orders food and the haunting begins. After a while, Barry shows up, claiming to be the owner of the house (219). He wants to solve his brother's murder, which suggests he is Simon Fevre.

They begin to eat and Ms. Heath enters.

Jack Vance: The idea of self-growing houses is central to "The Houses of Iszm" (1954).

Geography: The travel in Ms. Heath's flitter starts at 10 AM. Smithe and Buck are dropped off at the growing house not more than an hour before winter sunset (215), estimated at 5 PM. If they flew east, they would enter later time zones: 10 AM USA Eastern Seaboard would be 2 PM in Portugal and Ireland, 4 PM in Germany. Add time for travel. By this thinking, the growing house seems to be located somewhere between Portugal or Ireland and Germany.

Anomalies: Smithe says he saw "them carrying out your body

[. . .] Doctor" (219). While Smithe seems emotionally charged with the telling, the statement is in direct contradiction with the text given before.

Blurry Version: This Dr. Fevre seems a little lost. Perhaps he is a ghost who is not aware of his death, or is denying it. He might not be aware of which house he is in. Dead or alive, he might be thinking he is his brother Simon (referred to as "Mr. Fevre" (221)). Are Barry and Simon twins, perhaps?

Onomastics: The possible "Simon" here certainly matches the "Wavering" sense of the name.

Haunted House Details: Creatures materialize and dematerialize. This reportedly happened at Adah's house, with the ghost dog, but it also happened at the Polly's Cove Library, with the girl in white. Here Smithe seems to witness it happening with the "new Fevre" (220).

20. Night and Day (223–31)

Ms. Heath asks if they have seen a ghost. Smithe says he does not think so.

Ms. Heath denies she rented Smithe about any ghosts, but to solve a mystery. She says the mystery is threefold: What is the treasure hidden here? Where is it? Why was it hidden?

The deal she offers is that she will claim both reclones Smithe and Buck were lost, and they will live in this house, free to come and go at will (225). Until then, they are to sleep in the house's library.

In the night, Smithe finds himself sleepwalking. He goes through a door to the outside, and it locks behind him. Hiking around the house, he is followed by a dog, which he greets. His watch chimes one o'clock. He asks the dog for a way to enter the house, then follows the dog through a dog door, into a weird room (227), where Buck catches him.

Back on his shelf, Smithe dreams he is the older version, who had stolen a scalpel from Dr. Fevre and killed himself at Polly's Cove Library. Smithe feels himself drawn back by a woman's hand, and wakes in a sweat.

In the morning, Smithe talks Ms. Heath into checking out Audrey from the public library. They try, but she is already rented, so Ms. Heath puts a reserve on her.

The day goes by, and deep in the night, Smithe talks with Buck at a picnic table outside, away from the house's hearing. They touch on how their patron might try to betray them if they succeed in finding the treasure. Buck says that in that case he will murder her and escape into the Badlands. Then, as dawn approaches, they go in search of the kitchen.

Hammett: Interesting that Ms. Heath is pushing the ghost line, and Smithe is resisting it, even though it is genuinely spooky. This is in contrast to *The Dain Curse*, where the theme calls for a Lovecraft approach but Hammett cannot deliver spooky.

Alchemy: The weird room (227) at first seems like an art room, a room set up for a painting, but there is a supernatural element to it. There is a golden harp with a hundred strings (where usually the number is 47); a snarling thing in a cage; a double-sized statue of a bearded man with a woman's breasts, a figure that moves; and a painting on an easel, perhaps capturing this scene as a still life. (Note the importance of a harp in a house where dwells a person named "Harper.")

However, this impression is challenged by the flickering fire at the center of the room. Somehow this detail tips the scales from "art" toward "magic" or "alchemy." The hermaphrodite is certainly a symbol of alchemy.

Commentary: The new deal offered by Ms. Harper Heath is just like the old deal offered by Dane van Petten in *A Borrowed Man*.

When Ms. Heath, Smithe, and Buck go to the public library, one assumes their destination is the Polly's Cove Library and they are using the flitter again. On the way back, though, Smithe reveals they are in a groundcar (231). Not really an anomaly, just a fakeout.

21. A New Fevre (232–36)

In the morning, Smithe and Buck find Rose at a table. Smithe says he is the one who rode in the trailer with her and Millie, but she does not seem to be the one he knew: either she is a brand new reclone or she has somehow had a memory wipe. Dr. Fevre pulls up a chair. Smithe tells Rose that Dr. Fevre's wife checked him out and he will soon be overdue. Rose refers to herself as "the most recent edition at present" (233).

Smithe talks to this new Rose about the reclone life of being useful to fully humans and being burned.

Prompted by this, Dr. Fevre uses a screen to call the public library. He states he is the husband of Adah, who checked out Smithe, and he extends the rental period for two weeks. Then he asks Smithe what he knows about the treasure.

Smithe says, "Only that we found it and you have it" (234).

Dr. Fevre wants Smithe "to find out what it does, and how it can be made to do it safely, either in my company or in my absence" (234). As reward he offers a route for Smithe to buy himself out, an even better deal than before.

Rose reveals a memory of traveling in the trailer with Smithe, shifting her status or condition. She asks how he arrived at the growing house. He tells her a bit, and asks if she knows the doctor is married.

Rose says, "Yes. She'll be shocked to find me alive" (236). But then, after they discuss Adah's emotional cycle, Rose says, "I can only hope she'll be pleased."

Anomalies: Smithe says to Rose and Dr. Fevre that Dr. Fevre's wife checked him out (233), but it was Ms. Harper Heath who most recently rented him. Yet this might be Smithe stringing the "new" Fevre along again, and it works.

Blurry Version: This Rose seems as blurry as the doctor was a few chapters before. She flickers between stranger and old friend; between thinking she is fully human, and knowing the hard life of a reclone through experience. In other words, her condition seems rather like Adah's.

Solaris: The strangeness seems similar to the science fiction novel *Solaris* (1961) by Stanislaw Lem, in which the research base on an alien planet initially seems haunted by human ghosts that have an odd blurry quality of being not quite right.

Commentary: Barry seems strangely solicitous, in a way that might have made more sense back at the ice cave. Here it seems odd, almost an anomaly.

Rose's comment that Adah will "be shocked to find me alive" might suggest that Adah thinks Rose is dead. Since Adah is violently jealous, perhaps Adah tried to kill Rose, and thinks she succeeded.

22. Unburied Treasure (237–38)

Smithe meets Audrey, but she is a different one from the one he knew. He professes his love for her. She grabs the green box but he snatches it from her, "and reality reeled" (238).

Blurry Version: Audrey is blurry.

Pinocchio: Smithe's declaration of love is electrifying. He seems to have become a real person, achieving the Pinocchio goal. His love for Arabella is "hardwired," which makes it coerced, and in addition he knows that the original Ern/Arabella marriage dissolved after two years, so he is hardwired for that specific heartache. But Audrey is a real relationship. Even though at the beginning of his relationship with Audrey it feels like he is cheating on Arabella, the situation evolves over time.

Hammett: Smithe's declaration is very much like Sam Spade's last conversation with Brigid O'Shaughnessy near the end of *The Maltese Falcon*, but where Spade ultimately says, "I won't play the sap for you," Smithe goes the other direction.

Commentary: What Smithe says seems emotionally true and it seems to make him incredibly vulnerable, but he is using this open display of weakness as a tool to draw the enemy out, just as he used techniques in the previous novel to draw the enemy out. And it seems to have worked in this case, because when this Audrey grabs the green box, she does not seem like the Audrey who had returned the box to him at the cottage in the cavern, nor does she seem like the Audrey he had interviewed at the Polly's Cove public library, which means she does not seem like an authentic Audrey at all.

Orpheus: The scene with Smithe and a new Audrey re-enacts

the moment when Orpheus fails in his quest to rescue Eurydice from the underworld.

Wolfeana: The scenario of a couple who meet and then go on a self-directed adventure by boat (wherein they fall in love) has two cases in the New Sun milieu alone. The first case is Foila's tale, "The Armiger's Daughter," the fifth suitor's story in *The Citadel of the Autarch* (1983). The other is begun when Eata meets Maxellindis in *The Citadel of the Autarch,* later told to the end in "The Map" (1984; collected in *Endangered Species*).

Clark Ashton Smith: Perhaps the green metal box has an analog to a quested-after "brazen book" within lines 27–37 of the poem "The Hashish Eater":

> But naught deters me from the goal ordained
> By suns, and aeons, and immortal wars,
> And sung by moons and motes; the goal whose name
> Is all the secret of forgotten glyphs,
> By sinful gods in torrid rubies writ
> For ending of a brazen book; the goal
> Whereat my soaring ecstasy may stand,
> In amplest heavens multiplied to hold
> My hordes of thunder-vested avatars,
> And Promethèan armies of my thought,
> That brandish claspèd levins.
>
> (*Ebony and Crystal,* 1922)

The brazen book does not appear again in the poem, but near the end, the narrator announces a quest for a golden gorget bearing upon it the strange similarity of gemstone-writing:

> I am page
> To an emperor who reigns ten thousand years,
> And through his labyrinthine palace-rooms,
> Through courts and colonnades and balconies
> Wherein immensity itself is mazed,
> I seek the golden gorget he hath lost,
> On which, in sapphires fine as orris-seed,
> Are writ the names of his conniving stars
> And friendly planets. Roaming thus, I hear
> Like demon tears incessant, through dark ages,

The drip of sullen clepsydrae; and once
In every lustrum, hear the brazen clocks
Innumerably clang with such a sound
As brazen hammers make, by devils dinned
On tombs of all the dead; and nevermore
I find the gorget

This shifting, phantasmal quality seems especially relevant to the final chapters of *Interlibrary Loan.* The mazey palace seems a perfect match for the growing house that Smithe wanders through. The sought-after goals that transform in the non-logic of dreams, whether it be as physical as an alien artifact or as spiritual as a transformational love.

APPENDICES TO
INTERLIBRARY LOAN

Appendix ILL1: Back to the Beginning Overture
Smithe's Proustian overture at the beginning includes four
touchstones: the Spice Grove Public Library; the patter of
Chandra's black Mary Janes; Audrey the lady captain, who had
loved and accepted Smithe; and Dr. Fevre and his brother.

△△△

That Smithe has returned to the Spice Grove Public Library
means that he did not accept the Heath deal nor the new Fevre
deal, just as he did not accept the van Petten deal in *A Borrowed
Man*. Presumably Smithe solved the Fevre threat by neutralizing
it.

The patter of Chandra's black Mary Janes is complicated. We
associate this with the later sound of high heels on a floor above,
but Mary Janes are not usually high heels, so there are probably
two different pairs of shoes going on. (Of the eight other women
are in the house, only the younger women, Idona, Ricci, and Rose,
are likely to be wearing high heels. However, the wearer of high
heels is probably a ninth woman, Ms. Harper Heath, and she is
acquiring Ricci from Barry's estate at that moment.) Chandra is
one of Smithe's two simultaneous patrons, and that he mentions
her here might suggest that in the end he served her interests
rather than the interests of Adah, her mother.

Audrey the lady captain, who had loved and accepted Smithe,
turns out to be very important. In the overture, Smithe does not

mention her in any forward-looking way, so it seems likely she is dead.

Dr. Fevre and his brother. Barry is central to the mystery, but his brother Simon is in the category of "seems important, yet invisible," along with Adah's housekeeper Mrs. Snow, at least.

Appendix ILL2: Time and Money

Timeline

30 years ago: Barry's estimate of when Ricci and Idona died (162).

15 years ago: Possible date when Barry killed someone, and Adah knows (117); Barry and Adah get married, three years before pregnancy.

12 years ago: Chandra born; date later confused by Adah with Barry's first trip to Lichholm.

10 years ago: Possible date when Barry killed someone, and Adah knows (117).

7 years ago: Barry's sabbatical, first trip to Lichholm. Chandra, age 5, left behind in High Plains; Adah loses Barry, gets book with map.

5 years ago (guess): The events of *A Borrowed Man,* based on publication dates and Millie's "every year" line (15).

2 years ago: Mrs. Heuse reclone declared lost, secretly living at Adah's house (59).

This year: Barry's sabbatical.

5 weeks ago: Adah rents older Smithe (42).

Day 1: Smithe, Rose, and Millie shipped out in newer truck from Spice Grove. Older Smithe returned to Polly's Cove (42).

Day 2: Arrive at Niagara, shipped out in older truck.

Day 5: After three nights out, Smithe, Rose, and Millie arrive at Polly's Cove. Millie meets Chandra; Millie sees ghost girl in white.

Day 7: On third day, Chandra rents Smithe . . . Smithe goes to the library to find recruits for the sea voyage (Chapters 3, 4, 5, and 6).

Day 8: Smithe recruits Audrey Hopkins.

Day 8–14: Prep time for expedition.

Day 15–17: Travel time to meeting lugger; on the third day, Barry comes onboard.

Day 18: Arrive at Lichholm (120).

Day 19: Go to ice cave.

lacuna

Almost a week to return by lugger to Polly's Cove. Smithe and Audrey to library; Rose, Millie, Idona, and Ricci to Adah's house.

lacuna

Chandra rents Audrey.

lacuna

Friday: Barry murdered at Adah's house.

Monday: Chandra rents Smithe; at the house, Ricci says the place is haunted, having seen a strange shadow. Smithe hears high heels walking upstairs (possibly Ms. Harper Heath buying Ricci from Barry's estate). In the night, Chandra yells about somebody under her bed (181).

Tuesday: Night of the intruder.

Wednesday: Smithe and Audrey return to library.

Saturday?: Audrey checked out by a strange man.

Tuesday?: Ms. Harper Heath rents Buck Baston for her haunt problem, which arrived with Ricci at the growing house.

Next Saturday?: Smithe checked out by K. Turner.

Sunday?: Smithe and K. Turner visit other world.

Monday?: Smithe and K. Turner return. Chandra returns Smithe to library.

Tuesday?: Smithe checked out by Ms. Harper Heath; talks with a blurry Barry.

Wednesday?: Smithe persuades Ms. Heath to rent Audrey, but Audrey is already rented out, so she puts a hold on the reclone.

Thursday?: Smithe talks with a blurry Rose.

Friday?: Smithe talks with a different Audrey.

lacuna

Day Alef: Smithe begins writing this adventure, probably completing one chapter a day.

Day Tav (guess): Smithe completes his writing after 22 days.

Internal Chronology of Composition

In contrast to *A Borrowed Man,* its sequel *Interlibrary Loan* shows no markers regarding the passage of time in the frame tale, nor any suggestion that the first chapter was written last. Without these markers, the text flows as if written that way and in that order. This time, then, the overture is a guide to Smithe on what he will write, rather than a reflection upon what he has already written.

Money

Ship rental: 1,300 creds for seven days, then 100 creds for each additional day (90).

Appendix ILL3: The Mystery of the Older E. A. Smithe

From Chapter 5, Smithe goes through stages of wondering if the older version killed himself or was murdered by Barry. By the beginning of Chapter 13, he is convinced it was suicide (169). Smithe does not say how he reaches this conclusion, but he does go through details on why it would not make sense. In the dream of Chapter 20, he says the older one had stolen a scalpel from Dr. Fevre and killed himself at the Polly's Cove Library.

According to Smithe's reasoning, it makes no sense for Barry to kill the older reclone in a public place. On the other side of the ledger, we ask what sense it would make for the reclone to kill himself right there and right then, and it seems to be in order to send a message to our Smithe.

The older Smithe seems to have gone to Spice Grove to investigate Barry; seen him cavorting with rented Rose and Millie; stolen a scalpel; and returned to give Adah the report on her husband's whereabouts and activities. Adah mutilated him and returned him to the library. While he is sitting there on the bargain bench, he sees a new Smithe arrive, along with Rose and Millie. Another day while he is sitting there, Barry comes in and rents both Rose and Millie. If the older Smithe is still alive when Barry comes by on his way out, Barry might well buy him and kill him out of sight later (just as Smithe outlines); if Smithe kills himself, Barry will leave the library without him, but the new Smithe will be on his trail.

Perhaps when Adah talks with the new Smithe, she leans more heavily upon the "find the island" part, to avoid the disappointment of a detective finding her philandering husband. That is, Adah's real goal has always been to find the treasure, not the husband.

Appendix ILL4: Return to the Doctor of Fishbowl Mountain

The novella "The Doctor of Death Island" continues to show a strong relation to Smithe's narrative: the "book as key" appears again; "Death Island" appears as Lichholm, and the doctor there is Barry; the murderously jealous girlfriend Jessica is the murderously jealous wife Adah; the name "Barry," for Barry Siegle and Barry Fevre; the man with a harem is Alvard in one and Barry Fevre in the other; and finally, an ambiguous ending.

The novella also contains an unexpected link to *Treasure Island,* through the mangled hand of Dr. Margotte. In the early chapters of *Treasure Island,* Black Dog, a pirate with a mangled hand, starts the adventure rolling in a frightening encounter with the boy-hero Jim Hawkins.

These connections between "The Doctor of Death Island" and both Smithe novels increase the likelihood that the Smithe novels are the perfected heirs of the abandoned Wolfe novel *In Grayhame Prison.*

For all of these reasons, a section by section synopsis of the novella is in order.

△△△

"The Doctor of Death Island" synopsis

0. Opening quote from *Oliver Twist* by Dickens.
1. A couple of prisoner orderlies talk about Alvard, who "left" two years ago.
2. Perhaps a year into his prison sentence, Alvard writing about stomach pain and having recently met a new 19-year-old, a prisoner who became the older orderly in the previous section.
3. Dr. Baldwin and Dr. Margotte interact in the prison hospital. Margotte has bulging eyes and a mangled hand. An orderly says Margotte is the doctor who is present at the time of death.
4. Alvard dreams a nightmare mixing his business partner Barry with the "angel of death" Dr. Margotte.
5. A newspaper clipping about Alvard's cryogenic freezing, for medical reasons, after two years of prison.

6. Alvard awakens.

7. Alvard's counselor, a female prisoner, tells him he is cured of his cancer. He is effectively immortal, and it has been forty years since his freezing.

8. Alvard gets up in the dim and explores a bit. He remembers the ceramic mountain in the too small fish bowl, an ornament which he named "Death Island."

9. The next day the counselor brings him a Bible. He tells her he invented speaking books. She leaves his file with him and he talks with it.

10. The next day, the counselor visits at breakfast. He will have three visitors.

11. Alvard wakes near midnight. An orderly says he probably slept through visitation time. In the morning he has roof time with the orderly. He learns he will not be released. He sees the towering new wall.

12. Point of view shifts to Jessica as she enters the prison to visit. This time without the girl.

13. Alvard has a dream that Dr. Margotte is coming to get him with the deadcart.

14. An orderly brings him breakfast. He thinks on his mother as Little Nell (from *The Old Curiosity Shop*), with a bit of singing Dora (from *David Copperfield*). He determines he is a prisoner of Death Island. He sees a dead sky-hulk drift by, enigmatic and incomprehensible.

15. Alvard in a wheelchair is taken down for visitors.

16. Jessica's side of their visit. Lisa, the girl, is her clone. Jessica talks about her old jealous nature. They never married. She will send Lisa as her sex-surrogate.

17. Jessica's gift to Alvard is a book of selections from the novels of Dickens. Alvard has stolen a knife, and he sharpens it.

18. Alvard walks into the visiting room, no longer needing a wheelchair. He tells his lawyer he will be released in months or weeks, but won't give details.

19. Megan, his counsellor, offers Alvard a bunk in her cell. There are two men there already. Opening a book reveals the text

is being corrupted by another text, the ending lines of *Bleak House*, Chapter 21, which has a strange relevance to Alvard's moment with a powerful woman.

20. Alvard meets the warden, a woman, and a strange man named Lon Matluck. They want him to do research, but he refuses unless he is first freed. He explains he killed his partner Barry Siegle for thinking he was the real creator of Alvard's invention. The sight of Barry's bulging eyes as he fell to his death haunts him.

21. Alvard is put in a punishment cell. He reflects upon how he worked the knife on the Dickens book. One day a guard delivers two letters, but he also suggests that Dr. Margotte is asking after him. This shakes Alvard, since Margotte must have died many years before.

22. The two letters. One is from Matluck, the other from Lisa and Jessica. Included is a talking card from Lisa, but it is corrupted by another text. Alvard identifies the invader as Miss Snevellicci (from *Nicholas Nickleby*). Alvard feels like Mephistopheles (the demon from the German legend of Faust), presumably because the Dickens characters seem to report to him on his situation like spirits.

23. The Presidential Center is floating in the air six kilometers up, tethered to the ground by elevator tubes. Alvard meets the (male) President and (female) Dr. Pomme. The problem they face is the invasion of Dickens characters, a "social disease of books." Over the last forty years, the country has become functionally illiterate.

24. Riding down the glass elevator afterward with Dr. Pomme and Brenda Yarwood, a blonde woman who quickly seduces Alvard. After the elevator, Alvard and Brenda are arm-in-arm, heading down the ziggurat stairs, toward Jessica's car waiting at the base. A white-haired man comes running up. It is Dr. Margotte. Jessica shoots or not, and Alvard falls, hearing a scene from *Oliver Twist* where murder is called out, prompting Bill Sikes to flee. It seems that Barry has been avenged by Dr. Margotte.

ΔΔΔ

The fact that the second Smithe novel continues to reference "The Doctor of Death Island" adds further heft to the notion that the two are a reworking of Wolfe's stalled novel *In Grayhame Prison* (Wright's *Shadows of the New Sun*, p. 23), a work which had probably birthed "The Doctor of Death Island." The Faust elements, the "people from books" idea, even the Buck Rogers details, are refined and strengthened.

Appendix ILL5: The Faust File

Faust is the main character of the famous German legend about a scholar who sells his soul to the Devil for a life of unlimited knowledge and worldly pleasures. Englishman Christopher Marlowe made a play on it circa 1587. German Goethe wrote another play two hundred years later. Russian Bulgakov wrote his version as a novel in the 20th century.

Each of these three forms has details of difference. Take the example of female companions for Faust: in Marlowe's play, Faustus conjures up Helen of Troy, the legendary beauty of ancient texts, and keeps her as a lover; Goethe's play has peasant girl Gretchen (short for Margarete), who has Faust's baby out of wedlock; while Bulgakov's adultress Margarita learns to fly like a witch in order to rescue her Faust.

Wolfe-scholar Robert Borski traces Faust in Wolfe's novel *Peace* with "The Devil His Due" (collected in *The Long and Short of It*). Wolfe's novella "The Doctor of Death Island" makes direct allusion to Faust. Both of these cases cast Faust as the main character.

Interlibrary Loan also has a Faustian character, but instead of Smithe it is Barry. Looking through this lens makes Smithe into an avenging angel or demon, one who will take Barry's soul to Heaven or Hell.

Barry seems a bumbling Faust. From his version, he and then-intern Peggy discovered a technique for reviving the frozen dead. If we assume the resurrection is due to the proximity of the green box alone, then we might suppose the "technique" is more a "location" within the invisible radius of the hidden box's "life field radiation." Perhaps, having stumbled upon the fact that frozen corpses brought to this one isolated area of the caverns causes the corpses to revive, Barry then built his ice house exactly there. As a result, if he finds any nubiles among the dead, he can haul them to the ice house for their awakening.

Barry has a harem, including multiple Margaretes. Adah is Goethe's Gretchen, who has the baby. Peggy is Bulgakov's Margarita, who flies to Faust's rescue. Rose is Marlowe's Helen of

Troy, a spirit raised from a book to be his concubine. The teen angels Ricci and Idona are fresh new Gretchens to bear his future children.

The Faust stories have a variety of endings: sometimes Faust goes to Hell, and sometimes he goes to Heaven. Barry's fate in *Interlibrary Loan* is uncertain, but then, he is not the main character, Smithe is, and the idea of Smithe as an uncertain angel/demon finds solid traction in Smithe's internal debate over the guilt of Barry in the death of the older Smithe. In Chapter 8 he is wrestling with it; in Chapter 13 he finds Barry innocent. But then Barry is murdered, and Smithe is railroaded by Officer Turner into finding his killer, at which point Smithe wrestles with his conscience again, as well as wrestling bodily with Turner herself.

Appendix ILL6: The Dain Curse

Among Dashiell Hammett's five novels, *The Dain Curse* is widely seen as the weakest and least effective. It is the "spooky" case, which is why I immediately thought of it when *Interlibrary Loan* began hinting at the supernatural in Chapter 2, but in hindsight the influence of "The Dain" shows up much earlier, all the way back in *A Borrowed Man*.

At the beginning of Hammett's novel, the Continental Op is hired by an insurance company to investigate a crime of stolen diamonds. The gems were low grade, flawed in color: they were on loan to a scientist, Edgar Leggett, who was experimenting on a method to improve their color (hinting at alchemy). They were stolen from a locked cabinet in the laboratory on the third floor of his house.

In the opening paragraph, the Continental Op finds a diamond on the front lawn. He gives it to the scientist, who identifies it as one of the missing eight stones. Looking over the crime scene, the detective quickly figures that the robbery was an inside job, and that the lawn gem was planted there.

The scientist shares the house with his wife and their twentyish daughter, Gabrielle. By Chapter 6, the scientist is dead by apparent suicide, but it looks like the wife did it, just as it was the wife who directed the stealing of the diamonds, and then killed the thief.

These elements map to the first E. A. Smithe novel, *A Borrowed Man*. There is a house with a laboratory with gems under lock. In *A Borrowed Man*, when Conrad returns to Earth and finds his safe has been looted, he discovers it was an inside job. He kills his son for the theft, and in turn is murdered by his own daughter.

That gems are involved, with a hint at alchemy, matches the suspicions late in the novel that Conrad was synthesizing the emeralds.

That the inside job was by a relative is another similarity.

The first name of Dane van Petten might be a phonetic allusion to the family name of "Dain" in *The Dain Curse*.

When Smithe gives Dane the one emerald remaining of the

seven, at the end of the case, he is mimicking the way that the Continental Op gives the scientist the lawn diamond remaining of the eight at the beginning of the case.

The Dain Curse is made up of three parts, and the second part, "The Temple," is where things get spooky. The Continental Op, trying to protect Gabrielle Leggett, goes up against a ghost, so this vaguely tracks how Smithe tries to protect Chandra in dealing with the apparitions of *Interlibrary Loan,* beginning in Chapter 2.

Interlibrary Loan has the mysterious Ms. Harper Heathe, who rents Smithe and takes him to parts unknown. In *The Dain Curse,* Gabrielle has mysterious friends Mr. and Mrs. Harper. The scientist tells the Continental Op why his daughter is not available for questioning: "Friends of hers, a Mr. and Mrs. Harper, drove up from Los Angeles and asked her to go along on a trip up in the mountains" (*Dain,* Chapter 4: "The Vague Harpers"). This turns out to be a lie: Gabrielle is in town, at the cultish temple.

In this way, two-thirds of *The Dain Curse* have a marked influence upon both *A Borrowed Man* and *Interlibrary Loan.*

Appendix ILL7: Niven's "Gil the Arm"

Larry Niven's "Gil the Arm" is one of the more successful science fiction detectives. His main job is catching "organleggers," criminals who chop up victims for the body-part black market.

There are a number of background details in Gil's world that are opposite to the situation in Smithe's world: Gil's world is overpopulated at 18 billion, but Smithe's world is in population decline; Gil's world has slower-than-light star drives, but Smithe's world has no star drives; Gil's world has established a number of star colonies in "Known Space," but Smithe's world has no star colonies.

With that out of the way, consider a few points of congruence.

The story "ARM" (1975) features flying cars, flying taxis, and flying patrol cars that are fairly standard to genre, but strongly similar to the vehicles in *A Borrowed Man*.

"Death by Ecstasy" (1969) begins with the mysterious death of a friend. At a certain point Gil wonders if his friend committed suicide to send a message to Gil, which tickles at the mystery in *Interlibrary Loan* about the death of the older Smithe as a message-bearing suicide.

"The Defenseless Dead" (1973) opens in a cryogenic facility that seems very similar to Cadaver Island in *Interlibrary Loan*. The keeper gives Gil a brief tour: the earliest cases are accident victims, followed by the insane. The facility is only at two-thirds capacity, and the two men talk about the fad of the Freezeout Kids, young people who froze themselves for a better future. Unfortunately, the world needed body parts for the living, so they voted to give themselves the parts of the Freezeout Kids, "And a third of the world's frozen dead, twelve hundred thousand of them, had gone into the organ banks." As the story begins, the UN is talking about a second freezer law, only three years after the first one, this time targeting the insane, amounting to 300,000 bodies.

This highlights an important detail of similarity between the visions of Niven and Wolfe: The commodification of people. Even though Niven's world has overpopulation and Wolfe's has underpopulation, both societies reach for immortality in ways which seems to require a subhuman class.

Appendix ILL8: Worlds and Wonders

An attempt to sketch out the various worlds and wonders of the text.

Worlds

The dim, disquieting world of Smithe's green square vision. This world appears to be an infernal paradise, where the prostitute, the lech, and the pimp eternally enjoy their singular fixations. The three figures seem generic yet specific, like an illustration from an early *Dungeons & Dragons* booklet.

The jungle world of the green box reality shift. Smithe does not say it reminds him of the world he had visited before in *A Borrowed Man.*

The tree world of weird plants and the humanoid intruder via portal.

Wonders

The green square. The map is a magical artifact. It was drawn by some unknown person based upon a survey of Lichholm, and it marks the location of the treasure of the green box. Following the pirate logic, the green box had been stolen from elsewhere by humans or humanoids who then hid it on Lichholm, and they drew the map. Barry had acquired the map but, perhaps accidentally, he left it behind. Since Barry was mainly interested in cadavers, it worked out for him, but for this weird "resurrection" thing. Apparently, based upon Barry's degree of lecherous interest, a frozen corpse might spontaneously come to life. Truly a Faustian paradise.

Touching the green square gives a vision, which seems magical, but perhaps the map itself is the key to securing the treasure. Because notice that, when Smithe enters the cave with the map, the treasure guardian walks up and gives the green box to him, as if recognizing him as the bearer of the key, the rightful owner.

The ghosts. At first, with the girl in white at the library, it seems like the ghosts might be other-world tourists using a technology different than portals, a shortcut. But with the ghost dog at Adah's house, it seems as though the entity is being drawn by a living person's memory, in this case, the dog is a deeply rooted trauma of Mrs. Heuse. Since the only similar detail between the girl in white at the library and the ghost dog in the house is the presence of Chandra, it seems that she is the "spirit medium" and other people (perhaps Millie at the library, definitely Mrs. Heuse at the house) provide the call.

Then Ricci arrives at the house and sees strange shadows; when she is taken to the growing house, haunts erupt there. Following from the Chandra example, it appears that Ricci is the medium, and the ghosts appear from the anxieties of others, which would be Ms. Heath and then Buck Baston. Since Ricci is a revived corpse who can see ghosts, there is a hint that Chandra might also be a revived corpse (and her birth by Adah a lie); but there is also a suggestion that Chandra had caught her power from Adah (when Smithe thought it was an infectious paranoia schizophrenia (36)), so maybe Ricci caught the power from Chandra and/or Adah.

To this stage, all the sightings were by others, but when Smithe sees a haunt, other details come into play. Smithe was specifically trying to solve the mystery of Barry's death, and suddenly Barry appears at the growing house. Smithe lies to this Barry, and the ghost adjusts, just as if it were a conman playing along with the mark.

The green box. This artifact allows some sort of shortcut between at least two worlds: Earth and a jungle world. It might link to other worlds if turned in different ways.

The angels. Barry claims that he has discovered cryogenic revival, but the suspicion remains that the resurrection power comes from the obviously magical green box.

The competing team for the green box. The "other side" in the contest is very vague. Since they need help in using the green box, this suggests the green box did not originate with them. For a simple model, let's imagine the green box originated in the infernal paradise, and the competing team is on the tree world (with animal plants and the humanoids).

The other world assassin. The man with the feathered helm comes through the portal into Adah's house, he does not materialize and dematerialize like a ghost. He seems adept at tracking items left behind, like the big arrow.

The question is why he would kill Barry, and why at this time.

Appendix ILL9: Speculative Interpretation

The end of *Interlibrary Loan* seems abrupt. Revisiting the overture at the beginning of Chapter 1 gives a few strong suggestions about the end state. The exercise remaining is one of filling in the gap between the end of Chapter 22 and the overture. In speculating, I will try to be mindful of what is necessary, what is highly probable, and what is less probable.

The necessary elements result in a return to the status quo ante: Smithe, from his cliffhanger at a location probably overseas, is safely returned to his familiar shelf at Spice Grove, east of the Rockies; from the potential of winning fully human independence, Smithe instead maintains his role as library property; and the access between the other worlds must be removed.

ΔΔΔ

The self-building house is an unusual thing. It might be one of Barry Fevre's houses. It might be a regular technology of Earth, or it might be an alien lifeform from another world, perhaps a beachhead of alien invasion.

The blurry versions of characters seem to be reanimated puppets, like second-rate pod people from *Invasion of the Body Snatchers* (1956), or the ghosts of Lem's *Solaris*. The text gives us that the man in the feathered helm killed Barry, and then a blurry Barry shows up at the growing house, perhaps suggesting a connection between killing and puppetry. This could be extended to Rose, who seems blurry at the growing house, and thus was perhaps murdered (by Adah, in this case); then there is Smithe's Audrey, who was checked out from Polly's Cove a week before he was, and thus was perhaps murdered.

Adah's scattered mind initially seems to be a natural condition, but in light of blurry Barry and blurry Rose, it seems increasingly likely that Adah herself is blurry, too. If she was murdered, then that might be the killing ten years ago that Smithe intuits.

The ghost dog haunting Adah's room seems to be drawn from Mrs. Heuse's troubled past. Because Mrs. Heuse is now herself a "pet" of Adah for the last two years, she is anxious. The way Adah mutilated the old Smithe must have made Mrs. Heuse even more apprehensive.

The girl in white was seen by Millie at the Polly's Cove library. Perhaps this is the same as Smithe seeing the blurry Barry at the growing house, since he had seen Barry before. So maybe the girl in white is known by Millie. Yet the library is not "haunted," so how is a materialization/dematerialization possible? One constant to the ghost dog and the girl in white is the presence of Chandra.

If the murdered become reanimated puppets, this might explain why the old Smithe would take his own life, to avoid such a fate.

Smithe seems to verbally fence with the blurry Barry, causing the blur to readjust in reaction. In their first encounter, Smithe says he saw Barry's dead body being carried out, and the blur reacts by suggesting that it is not Barry, but Barry's brother, Simon. The blur seems to think it owns the house it has materialized in, and Smithe does not correct it, letting it flip between talking about a niece and a daughter, as if flailing about for a clue. Smithe does a similar "mental judo" in talking with blurry Rose. In this fashion Smithe flourishes his Puss in Boots strategy, making the shapeshifters change to his subtle bidding, played to great effect with the blurry Audrey.

There are at least two worlds involved. In the beginning it seems like Barry is involved in some evil thing on the alien side, and his long-suffering wife Adah is the Earth side. Through the speculative reading I am spinning here, Barry is initially on the Earth side, avoiding Adah because she is a puppet of the other world, and her hiring of Smithe is really about finding the treasure, the green box, not about finding her husband Barry. What the text calls "the New Fevre" asks exactly these questions, essentially continuing the conversation started by Adah.

As for neutralizing threats, while there are a dozen locked

doors in that hallway of Adah's haunted house, it seems only one of them opens onto an alien world, which is simpler than the portal Smithe encountered at the Coldbrook house, where there was a window in addition to the door. Smithe would presumably treat the Adah house portal in the same way he treated the Coldbrook portal, by destroying the power source, and Smithe had identified the alien power source as being above the treehouse. Again, it seems simpler than the situation at the Coldbrook house: here, all Smithe has to do is start a raging fire in the treehouse, then go through the portal into Adah's house. When the fire knocks out the power source, the link will be broken. Smithe can test it by opening the door, or perhaps just sniffing at it.

The timing of the green box being moved and Barry's assassination suggest the two events are related. Perhaps Barry was safe at the ice cave as long as the map was not around. When Smithe surreptitiously brought the map into the cave, Sven gave him the box, and perhaps an alarm bell went off, setting the other world assassin to investigate.

Smithe gave the box to Audrey, and Audrey gave it back to him at the ice cottage. Since this happened in front of everybody else, Barry presumably took possession of it at that time. Shortly thereafter, Barry, Adah, Prof. Pepper, and Chandra few away in the flitter.

At the time of Barry's assassination a few weeks later, it seems that he was staying at Adah's house with Adah, Audrey, Chandra, Mrs. Heuse, Idona, Millie, Ricci, Rose, and Mrs. Snow. This seems unusual, since he had previously been avoiding Adah.

A few weeks after Barry's murder, Ms. Harper Heath hires Smithe to clear her haunted house, but after the "new" Fevre shows up, the job abruptly shifts to being about a hidden treasure: identifying it, locating it, and determining why it was hidden. When Smithe later tells Fevre, "[W]e found it and you have it" (234), the statement can clearly apply to the green box, which was found at the ice cave when Sven gave it to Smithe, and since Barry witnessed Audrey giving it back to Smithe, Barry likely took possession of it there. The growing-house job shifts a second time, into figuring out what the green box does, and how to make it perform safely with Fevre present or absent.

The leadership at the growing house does not seem to be the original owner of the green box, nor even the original pirate of the green box, at least judging by the questions which seem to be so basic. The "ghost" technology seems different from the portal technology. It seems as though the "ghosts" are the ones trying to find the treasure, and they use Earth people to do this. Following from this, then, it would seem that the pirates who hid the green box in the ice cave are from the tall tree world.

ΔΔΔ

While *Interlibrary Loan* has significant elements from Faust, Smithe himself is not Faust, and the final chapter reveals him to be Orpheus.

Using the Orpheus-lens resolves a number of ambiguities to the novel by fixing an emotional polestar guiding Smithe's motivation in writing this text: he is Orpheus mourning his failed attempt to rescue Eurydice from the Underworld. The final chapter marks the moment of his loss, the whole point of his writing this work, beside which his subsequent labor at eliminating the threat is all just distracting wetwork. If it is emotionally true that Smithe is Orpheus, then he cannot write another word past that point. As Smithe put it in the beginning:

> "Sometimes I do my best to think only of the good things—of the pure and shining things, because I know that destiny and the real world are not all dark. Love is more real than the longest river, and kindness means more than any mountain range." (7–8)

ΔΔΔ

The Orpheus reading here has an unexpected side-effect of addressing the final third of Hammett's novel *The Dain Curse*. Recalling that the first third had to do with the stolen gems (which translates into the plot of *A Borrowed Man*), and the second third was the spooky one with a ghost and the supernatural (which contributes to *Interlibrary Loan*), the final part is about curing young Gabrielle from her opioid addiction. While there is nothing supernatural about it, the Continental Op is trying to rescue Gabrielle from slavery to the dark god of addiction, which is disturbingly close to breaking her out of the Underworld. And the key to it is love.

According to this, Wolfe's Smithe novels are surprisingly anchored to the entire novel of *The Dain Curse* by Dashiell Hammett.

BIBLIOGRAPHY

Behrends, Steven. *Clark Ashton Smith: Starmont Reader's Guide 49.* 1990. [ABM Ch. 18]

Borges, Jorge Luis. "Death and the Compass." 1942. [ABM2]

Brewer, Craig. "A Curiously Conflicted Book" (review of *Interlibrary Loan*). Ultan's Library.

Buck Rogers. [ABM Ch. 4, Ch. 11, ABM3; ILL Ch. 18, ILL4]

Bulgakov, Mikhail. *The Master and Margarita.* 1967. [ILL Ch. 6, ILL5]

Bulwer-Lytton, Edward. *Zanoni.* 1842. [ABM Ch. 1]

Burroughs, Edgar Rice. *Pirates of Venus.* 1932. [ILL Ch. 16]

Carrol, Lewis. *Alice's Adventures in Wonderland.* 1865. [ILL Ch. 16]

Crowley, John. *Engine Summer.* 1979. [ABM Ch. 1]

Davidson, Michael. *The Karma Machine.* 1975. [ABM Ch. 1]

"Davy Lowston." (Ballad). [ILL Ch. 6]

Dickens, Charles. *Bleak House.* 1853. (DODI; ABM, 53) [ILL4]

———. *A Christmas Carol.* 1843. (ABM, 53)

———. *David Copperfield.* 1850. (DODI; ABM, 53) [ILL4]

———. *The Mystery of Edwin Drood.* 1870. (ABM, 53) [ABM Ch. 4]

———. *Nicholas Nickleby.* 1839. (DODI) [ILL4]

———. *The Old Curiosity Shop.* 1841. (DODI; ABM, 53) [ILL4]

———. *Oliver Twist.* 1839. (DODI x2; ABM, 53) [ILL4]

Eco, Umberto. *The Name of the Rose.* 1980. [ABM2]

Faust. [ILL Ch. 6, ILL4, ILL5, ILL8, ILL9]

Hammett, Dashiell. "Corkscrew." 1925. [ABM Ch. 1]

———. *The Dain Curse.* 1929. [ILL Ch. 2, Ch. 5, Ch. 20, ILL6, ILL9]

———. "The King Business." 1928. [ABM Ch. 1]

———. *The Maltese Falcon.* 1930. [ABM Ch. 1, Ch. 18, ABM2; ILL Ch. 22]

———. *Red Harvest.* 1929. [ABM Ch. 18]

———. *The Thin Man.* 1934. [ABM Ch. 7, Ch. 17, Ch. 18]

Heinlein, Robert A. *Tunnel in the Sky.* 1955. [ABM Ch. 12]

Invasion of the Body Snatchers. (Motion Picture). 1956. [ILL9]

Johnson, Samuel. *Lives of the Most Eminent English Poets, Volume 7.* 1779. [ABM Ch. 7]

Kuttner, Henry. *The Dark World.* 1946. [ILL Ch. 16]

Pinocchio. [ABM Ch. 10; ILL Ch. 22]

Piper, H. Beam. *Murder in the Gunroom.* 1953. [ABM Ch. 2]

———. The Paratime series. [ILL Ch. 16]

Poe, Edgar Alan. "Annabel Lee." (Poem). 1849. [ABM Ch. 1]

———. "A Cask of Amontillado." 1846. [ABM Ch. 18]

———. "The Fall of the House of Usher." 1839. [ABM Ch. 18]

Proust, Marcel. *Swann's Way.* 1913. [ABM Ch. 1]

Puss in Boots. [ABM Ch. 10, Ch. 17, Ch. 18; ILL9]

Smith, Clark Ashton. "The Charnel God." 1934. [ILL Ch. 11]

———. "The Dead Will Cuckhold You." (Play). 1951. [ILL Ch. 11]

———. "The Death of Ilalotha." 1937. [ILL Ch. 11]

———. "The Door to Saturn." 1932. [ABM Ch. 12, Ch. 18]

———. "The Dweller in the Gulf." 1932. [ABM Ch. 2]

———. "The Empire of the Necromancers." 1932. [ILL Ch. 11]

———. "The Hashish Eater, or the Apocalypse of Evil." (Poem). 1920. [ABM Ch. 18; ILL Ch. 3, Ch. 16, Ch. 22]

———. "The Isle of the Torturers." 1933. [ABM Ch. 2]

———. "Morthylla." 1953. [ILL Ch. 11]

———. "Necromancy in Naat." 1936. [ILL Ch. 11]

———. "The Seven Geases." 1934. [ABM Ch. 2]

———. "The Vaults of Yoh-Vombis." 1932. [ABM Ch. 2]

———. "Vulthoom." 1935. [ABM Ch. 2]

Stevenson, Robert Louis. *Treasure Island.* 1883. [ILL Ch. 5, Ch. 6, Ch. 18; ILL4]

Vance, Jack. "The Houses of Iszm." 1954. [ILL Ch. 19]

Virgil. *The Aeneid.* [ABM Ch. 2]

Wolfe, Gene. *Bibliomen.* 1984. [ILL Ch. 18]

———. "British Soldier Near Rapier Antiaircraft Missile Battery Scans For The Enemy." (Poem). 1984. [ABM Ch. 4]

———. "Civis Laputus Sum." 1975. [ABM4]

———. "The Doctor of Death Island." 1978. [ABM Ch. 1, ABM3; ILL Ch. 11, ILL4, ILL5]

———. *Exodus from the Long Sun.* 1996. [ILL Ch. 16]

———. "The Eyeflash Miracles." 1976. [ABM Ch. 13]

———. *In Grayham Prison.* Unfinished novel. [ABM3; ILL4]

———. "Oh God Mother I Want To Ride The Turtle's Back Again." (Poem). 1988. [ABM Ch. 4]

———. *Operation ARES.* 1970. [ABM Ch. 2, ABM3]

———. *Peace.* 1975. [ABM Ch. 1]

———. *The Shadow of the Torturer.* 1980. [ABM Ch. 5; ILL Ch. 11]

———. *Soldier of the Mist.* 1986. [ILL Ch. 18]

———. "A Traveler in Desert Lands." 1999. [ILL Ch. 11]

Wright, Peter (editor). *Shadows of the New Sun.* 2007. [ABM Ch. 4, ABM3; ILL Ch. 6, ILL4]

Wynn, James. "A Weird Mystery" (review of *A Borrowed Man*). Ultan's Library. [ABM Ch. 1]

△△△

Smithe Bibliography

Smithe, Ern A. *The Corpse Drank Wine.* (ILL, 148)

———. *Death on a Daybed.* (ILL, 148)

———. *The Ice-Blue Kiss.* (ABM, 33) (ILL, 147)

———. *Kill Mama Kill Papa.* (ILL, 147)

———. *The Lantern in the Library.* (ABM, 11)

———. *Men Mice and Murderers.* (ILL, 147)

———. *Men Who Kill.* (ABM, 106)

———. *Murder for Prophet.* (ILL, 147)

———. *Murder on Mars.*

———. *Murder's Good for Business.* (ILL, 147)

———. *Nine Dead Women.* (ABM, 241)

———. *When Will Murder End?* (ILL, 148)

———. *Who Killed Cock Robin?* (ILL, 185)

Smithe mentions two of his series sleuths, "Red Searcher" and

"Mrs. Jacoby" (*A Borrowed Man,* 112). Later he lists three series: a young model as a detective; an alligator hunter turned bounty hunter (perhaps this is Red Searcher); and a criminal who helps the police in order to defer his own arrest *(Interlibrary Loan,* 222).

BOOKS BY THIS AUTHOR

Gene Wolfe's The Book Of The New Sun: A Chapter Guide

A chapter-by-chapter guide to Gene Wolfe's "The Book of the New Sun," its sequel "The Urth of the New Sun," and four shorter works.

A Chapter Guide To Gene Wolfe's Latro Novels

A chapter-by-chapter guide to Gene Wolfe's Latro novels: "Soldier of the Mist," "Soldier of Arete," and "Soldier of Sidon." The three Latro books are arguably Gene Wolfe's most challenging work.

Gene Wolfe: 14 Articles On His Fiction

Ten essays and four reviews, originally published from 1993 to 2014, in "The New York Review of Science Fiction," "Foundation," "Extrapolation," "Ultan's Library," "The Magazine of Fantasy & Science Fiction," "The Internet Review of Science Fiction," "Quantum," and a chapbook on "The Fifth Head of Cerberus." Some of them are available for free online, but many are hard to find.

Roadside Picnic Revisited: Seven Articles On The Soviet Novel That Inspired The Film "Stalker"

A collection of essays and a book review relating to "Roadside Picnic," the Soviet science fiction novel by Arkady and Boris Strugatsky. Six of the pieces were originally published in "The New

York Review of Science Fiction," and the seventh is previously unpublished. The subject is the novel, and there is nothing about the movie beyond a brief mention.

www.ingramcontent.com/pod-product-compliance
Lightning Source LLC
Chambersburg PA
CBHW021134020426
42331CB00005B/772